VILLA PARK HISTORICAL PRESERVATION COMMISSION

P9-AOT-326

Registration Methods
for the
Small Museum

Third Edition

AMERICAN ASSOCIATION FOR STATE AND LOCAL HISTORY BOOK SERIES

Series Editor

Sandra Sageser Clark
Michigan Historical Center

Editorial Advisory Board

Robert R. Archibald, Missouri Historical Society
Lonnie G. Bunch, Smithsonian Institution
J. Kent Calder, Indiana Historical Society
Phillip Cantelon, History Associates, Inc.
Deborah Kmetz, State Historical Society of Wisconsin
George F. MacDonald, Canadian Museum of Civilization
Phillip Scarpino, Indiana University-Purdue University, Indianapolis
Constance B. Schultz, University of South Carolina
Lawrence J. Sommer, Nebraska State Historical Society
Bryant F. Tolles, Jr., University of Delaware

About the Series:

The American Association for State and Local History Book Series publishes technical and professional information for those who practice and support history and addresses issues critical to the field of state and local history. To submit a proposal or manuscript to the series, please request proposal guidelines from AASLH headquarters: AASLH Book Series, 530 Church Street, Suite 600, Nashville, TN 37219. Telephone: (615) 255-2971. Fax: (615) 255-2979.

About the Organization:

The American Association for State and Local History (AASLH) is a nonprofit educational organization dedicated to advancing knowledge, understanding, and appreciation of local history in the United States and Canada. In addition to sponsorship of this book series, the association publishes the periodical *History News*, a newsletter, technical leaflets and reports, and other materials; confers prizes and awards in recognition of outstanding achievement in the field; and supports a broad educational program and other activities designed to help members work more effectively. Current members are entitled to discounts on AASLH Series books. To join the organization, contact: Membership Director, AASLH, 530 Church Street, Suite 600, Nashville, TN 37219.

Registration Methods
for the
Small Museum

Third Edition

■

Daniel B Reibel

ALTAMIRA
PRESS

A Division of Sage Publications, Inc.

Walnut Creek ■ London ■ New Delhi

Copyright © 1997 by AltaMira Press, A Division of Sage Publications, Inc.
All rights reserved. No part of this book may be reproduced or utilized in any form or by any means, electronic or mechanical, including photocopying, recording, or by any information storage and retrieval system, without permission in writing from the publisher.

For information address:

AltaMira Press
A Division of Sage Publications, Inc.
1630 North Main Street, Suite 367
Walnut Creek, CA 94596

SAGE Publications Ltd.
6 Bonhill Street
London EC2A 4PU
United Kingdom

SAGE Publications India Pvt. Ltd.
M-32 Market
Greater Kailash 1
New Delhi 110 048 India

PRINTED IN THE UNITED STATES OF AMERICA

Library of Congress Cataloging-in-Publication Data

    Reibel, Daniel B
      Registration methods for the small museum / author, Daniel B
    Reibel. — 3rd ed.
        p. cm. — (American Association for State and Local History
    book series)
      Rev. ed. of: Registration methods for small history museums. 2nd
    ed., rev. ©1991.
      Includes bibliographical references and index.
      ISBN 0-7619-8904-8 (cloth). — ISBN 0-7619-8905-6 (pbk.)
      1. Museum registration methods.   I. Reibel, Daniel B
    Registration methods for small history museums. II. Title.
    III. Series.
    AM139.R44 1997
    069'.52—dc21   96-51217
                                    CIP

97   98   99   00   01   8   7   6   5   4   3   2   1

Production Services: Carole Bernard, ECS
Editorial Management: Erik Hanson

Contents

About the Author

Daniel B Reibel began his museum career at the Detroit Historical Museum in 1957, and one of his first jobs was to catalogue the lighting collection. He gained his experience with small museums as director of the Allen Count–Fort Wayne (Indiana) Historical Society. He then began a twenty-five-year career with the Pennsylvania Historical and Museum Commission, where he had a chance to work with the collections, including Old Economy Village, Landis Valley, and Washington Crossing Historic Park. He is presently the curator of the Old Barracks Museum and editor of the *Chronicle* of the Early American Industries Association. He is the author of numerous articles on museum subjects, including a chapter in *Registrars on Record*. He serves on the faculty of the Collection Care Training Program and is president of the Council of American Revolutionary War Sites.

Registration Methods for the Small Museum

The operative words in the title are *"Registration Methods"* and *"Small Museum."* Taking them in order, I will try to explain why I wrote this book.

Registration Methods

It is a standard plot situation in novels, where there are curators or museums, to find the museum character "cataloguing." This recognizes a vague public perception that museums have something to do with records. This is usually presented as something so arcane that only a museum professional could understand it. I once read a spy novel where the museum curator was a black-belt judo expert and an Olympic-class fencer (he kills someone with each of these skills) and is completely familiar with the international art market—but he still has time to spend cataloguing! Just what he is cataloguing is rather vague, but it sure impresses the heroine. It is no wonder that so many people are trying to get into the museum field.

Museums do have something to do with records. Objects themselves do not speak. Perceptions of what an object is and its history are written down by a human being. It is the museum's ability to create, maintain, and, most importantly, pass on this written knowledge to the next keepers, that makes them museums. I hope that this book helps define a registration system, what it ought to do, and how to achieve a real registration system; one that will withstand the scrutiny of the most meticulous accreditation team.

Small Museum

No one has ever successfully defined a small museum. The Small Museums Committee of the Mid-Atlantic Association of Museums once defined a small museum as one with a lone professional, but I have been in many museums with several professionals who thought of themselves as small.

I once attended a meeting where a curator from a very large museum was to give a slide talk. She brought several assistants to help her; surely not a characteristic of a small museum. When she could not load her carousel I offered to help, but she gruffly refused any aid and said, "'The Man' will be along shortly to set this up!" Sure enough, along came a technician in her crew who knew what to do. Ever since, I have always considered a small museum as one where "The Man" or "The Woman" was the one who was looking back at you in the mirror.

When I wrote the first edition of this book in 1977–78 there was a good possibility that a small museum would not even have a decent typewriter. Now, even the smallest museum has access to a computer that gives them potential to do things of extraordinary sophistication, particularly when compared with museum registration systems of even ten years ago. I thought that if I could help the small museum use the potential of modern devices it would further the goal of every museum having a well-registered collection.

Small need not mean poorly run. Small may mean that the size and complexity of the collection can be grasped very easily, and be of a dimension where even a small staff can handle it. From my experience with accreditation visits and MAP surveys, I can assure you that some large museums cannot always say the same. I thought that a book that would give the small museum a reachable goal was what was required.

Over nineteen years ago, when I wrote the first edition, there was a better than even chance that the small museum was run by volunteers. The professionals at the few museums with paid staffs would more than likely be untrained. There were few ways to get training, as there was very little literature and training courses were few and far between. Boards were unsophisticated and expectations were low. In 1962, when I asked my board for an electric typewriter, I was told I did not need one! Computers were around, but only a handful of museums had one. There were no standards until the accreditation program started in 1970.

What a change! A good percentage of small museums have professional staffs, who have access to many training opportunities and an extensive body of literature. Typewriters are obsolete and even the smallest museum probably has access to a computer. Boards are much more sophisticated and aware of their responsibilities. There are rather high standards and these become more sophisticated each day. Any book has to reflect these changes and I hope this one does.

My experience is all in history museums and this will give the book a slant, but I think this book will be useful to any professional. There are differences between types of museums. History collections are large, like some science collections, but need to store lots of data, like art museums. Science museums have a better taxonomy than history museums, and art museums hardly need a classification system at all. Other than that, the need to be able to preserve information, track the collection, and account for one's actions is the same for any type of museum.

The Third Edition

Sometime in 1975, at a meeting at Colonial Williamsburg, I ran into Paula Degan who asked me the difference between the registration systems of an art, science, and history museum. I did not know, but went home and thought about it. I eventually wrote her, describing the differences between several types of museums that I use in Chapter One. The outgrowth of that question was the first edition of this book.

When I discussed the differences between registration methods for different types of museums, I realized that almost all the literature on museum registration was written for art museums. Not only that, there was very little other material on "professional" subjects in print. I thought my book would correct that condition.

When I was writing the first edition of this book, I had a chance to read Robert Chenhall's book *Nomenclature for Museum Cataloging* while it was in page proofs. I believed that this book would give history museums another tool to raise standards. Whether Chenhall or I contributed anything to it, standards are certainly higher today than they were then.

All of the examples used in this book exist and are from my own observations. For example, when I use the illustration of a schoolhouse at one end of the county and a mansion at the other, they exist, and I have visited them and looked at their collections.

Forms not printed in the text are in Appendix C. They are referred to by their number, i.e., C-6 for the sixth form in Appendix C.

I would like to thank the late Bill Alderson for encouraging me to publish the first edition, and, of course, my wife Patricia who kept me at it.

One

What Is a Museum Registration System?

Grandma's Attic

If you have ever had a chance to go into grandma's attic, you would have seen all the once valuable things there that had been used and put aside. It would have been a special thrill if you had gone there with grandma herself. She could have told you that the old chair was her grandfather's and what wonderful things he did! She could have told you all about the people in the old photographs and identified everyone in her wedding picture. All the mysterious devices you had never seen before could have been explained to you. If you have ever experienced such an adventure, you would never forget it.

But what if grandma is not here? Who will bring this material to life? The chair would be just an old chair; the photographs would show strangers; the uses of the strange devices would remain unknown; grandma's wedding gown would be just an old dress carefully packed away. The objects are silent. They themselves do not speak, but grandma did. Grandma is the memory of these things. If it is not written down that memory will be lost.[1]

The museum registration system is the museum's memory. Long after curators and registrars have come and gone, the records of the museum will speak. In keeping the historical story straight, they are as important as the object itself. A museum that fails to keep good records fails in its primary function; some would say its only function. With good records, more than the object is preserved. With poor records, something more valuable than the object itself may be lost.

The person, or persons, in charge of a museum have been given a trust. They have been placed in charge of a collection for a little while. It is their obligation and duty to see that the collection is well cared for and that it is passed on to the next caretakers in as good a condition as when they received it. Good care includes good records. Good record keeping does not have to be difficult, time consuming, or costly.

There are collections of furniture, beer-bottle caps, art, matchbook covers, glass, ceramics, insulators stolen from telephone poles, seashells, animals, pornography, and so on. A museum may collect one or several of these things and more, but not all collections are museums. A museum has several characteristics that separate it from a mere collection:

- The museum is a nonprofit educational institution.
- The collection is educational or aesthetic in nature.
- The collection is created and maintained under strict standards.
- There is an assurance of continuity. A museum is an institution that will, theoretically, last forever.
- A museum, no matter how privately owned, is held in the public interest.
- A museum has a professional person,[2] knowledgeable about the collection, in charge of it. In order to meet this criteria, volunteer-run museums must find a person or committee who can develop the requisite knowledge and skills.

Private collections lack some or all of these characteristics. The American Association of Museums (AAM) defines a museum for accreditation purposes as:

". . . an organized and permanent nonprofit institution, essentially educational or aesthetic in purpose, with a professional staff, which owns and utilizes tangible objects, cares for them, and exhibits them to the public on some regular schedule."[3]

Notice the statement that the museum owns and cares for its collections. For accreditation purposes, care has been defined as protecting the essential integrity of the object and being able to account for it. The caring for collections is the essence of the difference between being a museum and not being a museum. The records are considered an important part of the object. Most museums that fail to be accredited fail because of the kind of care given their collections. Many such failures come about because of inadequate or incomplete records. A museum will be considered a good museum if the staff maintains good records, but it may not be considered a museum at all if that is not done.

Over the years, the museum field has developed a record-keeping system that is pretty standard and consistent enough to be applied to widely different circumstances of each museum collection. The system is actually quite simple. There is not much mystery to it, nor is there a need to invent your own record-keeping system.

How One Type of Museum May Differ from Another Type of Museum

There are differences between types of museums, and these are often reflected in their record-keeping procedures.

I must first define the term "specimen" to make the rest of this discussion clearer. This term helps explain the difference among museums better than any other. It comes from a Latin root meaning a distinguishing mark, with the idea that the object stands out. Technically speaking, any object in a museum collection is a specimen. However, in the narrower use of the term, as often used in the museum field today, a specimen is an object that represents any other object in its class or type. It may be the best example, but it is still just representative. To some museums, any specimen can easily be replaced by another, and better, one. Some museums separate their specimens from their collection, and even give the specimens a lower standard of care. This concept of the object as a specimen is not universal in the museum field, nor even popular, but it is something to keep in mind.

The major difference between a history museum and other museums is that they collect objects that have some historical association attached to it. This historical association makes the object valuable all out of proportion to its value as a specimen or its monetary value. *It cannot be replaced by a better specimen.* Other characteristics of history museums are that the collections are of objects that are made people and the collections tend to be large and monetarily valuable. History museums share many of these characteristics with art and anthropology collections, but normally a history museum is the only type of museum where the major collecting effort is of objects with historical associations. Other differences among museums will be discussed when we get to classification.

Registration systems in museums have to be flexible enough to account for these conditions and be able to record a lot of data on many objects.

Definitions

It is important to understand the terms used in this book, so I am listing some of them. My definitions are not exactly those of a dictionary, but they show the way these terms are commonly understood in the museum field today:[4]

Accession: An accession is an object or a group of objects in the museum collection obtained at one time from a single source. The act of accessioning is taking possession and title to the object, placing it in the museum collection, and making a record of it.[5]

Catalogue: A catalogue is a reference tool created by arranging some of the collection records in categories.[6]

Collection: A museum collection is a group of objects kept together for some reason. Usually the relationship is due to similarities in the nature of the objects; their being collected by an individual or group; or their association with a person, place, or event. A collection may have only a few pieces in it, or it may have thousands. A museum may contain one collection or several collections.

Curator: The definition of this term has been narrowed in the last few years, but for the purposes of this book the word means the professional person in charge of a collection. The collection may be the whole museum or only part of it.[7]

Director: This term has superseded the term "curator" to describe the person in charge of the museum. This term recognizes that the museum is not only its collections but its program. The director is not only in charge of the professional activities of a museum but its administration as well.

Documentation: This is the factual information gleaned about each object in the collection. Some of this information is developed by examination of the object and some is acquired by research.

Institution: This is the organization, whether historical society, association, museum, or some larger entity, that has the ultimate ownership and authority over the collection.

Ledger: The master record; one containing all the accession information. In manual systems, it is often a bound book. In computer systems, it is some utility in the program that can generate a master record.

Museum: This is an institutionalized collection, the records of that collection, the physical plant where this collection is housed, and is potentially accreditable as a museum by the AAM.

Object: This is intended as a generic term for the things in a museum collection. I am going to use the term in the singular as a convention. In history museums, most objects are made by one or more individuals.

Register: For our purposes, the register is a list of the accessions, loans, etc., of the museum in some logical order.

Registrar: This is the person in charge of the museum's registration system. In the past few years, the responsibilities of the registrar have been broadened to include extended responsibilities over the whole area of collection policy and management. In fact, the term "collection manager" is beginning to replace registrar in some museums as the preferred term. In museums without a registrar, the curator(s) or the professional staff are responsible for the records.[8]

Registration: This is the whole process of creating, acquiring, and keeping the records on a museum collection and is the subject of this book.

The person who is actually doing the registration should start with the attitude that registration is just one of the problems to be solved, so that some of the other problems, such as acquiring more objects, preserving existing objects, and interpreting the collection, can be taken care of.

Boundaries

The first thing needed for a good registration system is a firm set of boundaries for the museum.[9] This is found in the museum's statement of purpose and mission. These two are commonly combined into what is usually called the mission statement. The statement should say what the museum is, what it is going to do, how it is going to do it, and any limits on these actions. A typical statement might be:

Mission Statement
Hero County Historical Society

(*purpose*)
What Is the Museum?

The Hero County Historical Society is a nonprofit educational association

What Is Its Purpose?

Collect, preserve, and interpret the history of Hero County, Pennsylvania;

For What Time Period?

From the arrival of the first Native Americans in this region until the present day; with special emphasis on the period since the founding of the County (1785) until the end of the 19th century (1900);

(*mission*)
By What Means?

By the collection of books, documents, artifacts, and other cultural objects; preserving them; and interpreting them to the public by means of a museum, educational programs, lectures, public events and publications;

Any Other Qualifications?

To encourage others to collect, preserve, and interpret the history of Hero County; and do everything worthwhile to carry out our purpose.

Written as a paragraph, the statement would look like this:

Mission Statement
Hero County Historical Society

The Hero County Historical Society is a nonprofit educational association that collects, preserves, and interprets the history of Hero County, Pennsylvania; from the arrival of the first Native Americans in this region until the present day; with special emphasis on the period since the founding of the County (1785) until the end of the 19th century (1900); by the collection of books, documents, artifacts, and other cultural objects; preserving them; and interpreting them to the public by means of a museum, educational programs, lectures, public events and publications; and to encourage others to collect, preserve and interpret the history of Hero County; and do everything worthwhile to carry out our purpose.

This is a good mission statement since it confines the museum to the collection of only those objects related to the history of the county. That limit is very broad, as it allows the museum to collect almost everything.

As the museum's operation grows and changes over the years, the purpose will probably not change much, but the mission will become more and more complex. Large museums will have mission statements that cover several pages.

It is not unknown for a museum to rewrite their mission statement every time they develop a new long-term plan, say every five years. For the small museum, a simple mission statement, like the one above, will be perfectly adequate.

Before developing a collection policy, the museum should carefully examine its statement of purpose to see if it defines the kind of collection the museum wants. In the case of the one above, it would not limit the museum enough. This museum would want to develop a collections management policy statement that further defines the museum's mission:

Collections Management Policy
Hero County Historical Society

What Type of Objects Will the Museum Collect?

It is the policy of the Hero County Historical Society to collect only those objects made and/or used in Hero County; or that are associated with a person, place, or event in the County; or, to a limited extent, are typical or representative of objects made or used in the County;

What Is the Scope of the Collection?

and that are historical, cultural, or aesthetic in nature;

Is There a Limit on the Period of the Collection?

that cover the period from 1785 to 1900;

Are There Any Other Limits?

and for which the museum has an ultimate use; and for which the museum can care under standards acceptable to the museum field at large.

Written out as a paragraph, this statement would look like this:

Collections Management Policy
Hero County Historical Society

It is the policy of the Hero County Historical Society to collect only those objects made and/or used in Hero County; or that are associated with a person, place or event in the County; or, to a limited extent, are typical or representative of objects made or used in the County; and that are historical, cultural, or aesthetic in nature; that cover the period from 1785 to 1900; and for which the museum has an ultimate use; and for which the museum can care under standards acceptable to the museum field at large.

This statement directs the collection a little more narrowly than the statement of purpose. The object has to have a direct association with some person, place, or event in the county. The museum cannot collect seashells since they were not made or used in the county and are not historical, cultural, or aesthetic in nature. The museum cannot collect a locomotive, unless it will have some use for it and can take care of it. These conditions may not be too confining and they will keep the museum's collection activities concentrated on what it really needs and can care for.[10] The enforcement of such a policy will help prevent problems with deaccessions later.

These collection management policies keep the museum focused on what it is really trying to do. Before you develop any collection manual, you should make sure that your policies define a method of reaching your goals and that everyone understands them.

Collection Management Policy Manual

All the policies and procedures that affect the collection should be brought together in a collection management policy manual. The reason for having a manual is that there will be a consistent set of practices through several curatorial administrations. It is important that the manual reflect actual operating practices, be usable by anyone, and that it be short and easy to read. Collection management polices are not stagnant documents. They need to be reviewed annually and updated when needed.

Even the smallest museum needs legal advice as to exactly how the whole collection policy should be handled. It is a good idea to have the museum's whole collection policy looked over by a good lawyer.

The procedures carry out the policy and may require certain practices that affect policy. The manual should include both policies and procedures. The board should be involved in developing the manual and in carrying out its provisions. There are two sample collection management policies in the appendix.

What Does a Registration System Do?

After coming this far in the chapter, I should at least explain what a museum registration system does:

The registration system is a system of policies, procedures, practices, and documents that provides a link between the objects and their history and ensures that:

- The museum's right of ownership of the object is established.
- Associations with a person, place, or event are preserved.
- Interpretation of the object is enhanced.
- Preservation of the object is aided.
- The museum can identify and account for every object in the collection.

In order to do all these things, the museum must have a well-developed collection policy and a set of procedures to carry it out.

The Rule and Its Test

There is a rule that should apply to any museum registration system.

That rule is:

Any registration system used by a museum should be readily understandable to any intelligent but uninformed layman using the registration system itself, without any human assistance.

The museum does not need a high priest or priestess to interpret a divinely inspired registration system to the benighted masses below. It needs a system that anyone can understand in the event that the curator is not there to explain it.

The test of any system is:

The museum should be able to produce any object from its collection from any document picked at random from its registration system.

The museum should be able to produce all the documentation for any object picked at random from its collection.

If your museum cannot pass the test, keep working on the problem until you can. I have seen large museums with large professional staffs that cannot pass the test and small volunteer-run museums that can.

Who Bells the Cat?

There is almost always a board or governing body responsible for the museum. That group has the ultimate responsibility for the collection. The board decides who is actually going to do the work.

In a museum with a professional staff, the decision is much easier: the professional staff does the work. The board has delegated its responsibility for the area of the museum to the professional staff, and those persons, among other things, are responsible for the records. It does not matter how large the staff is; if the curator or director is the only paid professional, that person is responsible. In situations where there are more than one professional, the director may delegate responsibility. If the museum is fortunate enough to afford it, there will be a registrar, but do not get the chain of responsibility confused. The governing body is responsible and delegates its authority to the professional, who may further delegate it. If something goes wrong, it is the professional's responsibility. If the governing body allows the error to continue, it is their responsibility. With apologies to Lewis Carroll, what I have told you three times is true.

In the case of the volunteer-run museum, the governing board not only has the responsibility, but also has to do the work. In that event, there is usually a person or group of persons willing to undertake the care of the collections. This person or group becomes a directorate in place of a director. This directorate may be incorporated into a collections or museum committee. The committee takes charge of the registration system and reports to the governing body on its activities from time to time. These volunteer-run museums can have very effective records. Whether run by volunteers or professionals, a museum can have the kinds of records it wants. If the people involved in the museum have a commitment to a good registration system they will have it, whether or not there is a professional on the staff. Unfortunately, the opposite corollary is also true.

The collections committee of the governing body offers an extra bit of continuity and responsibility to the collection and can make the transition from one curator to another or from one administration to another more easily than it would otherwise be. For these reasons, I feel that museums should have some committee to oversee its collections, whether or not the museum has a professional staff.[11]

Where to Start

The ideal situation is not to have a previously assembled collection at all so you can start from scratch. New organizations are actually very fortunate in this respect. A new organization can develop a registrar's manual before it ever acquires a single object and can have an accurate and complete registration system from the beginning.

Museums that already have collections may not be so lucky. If your collection has been well cared for and you have good records, you are probably reading this book for the fun of it. If your collection has not been taken care of and the records are a mess, you have a problem to solve before you do anything else.

What to Do about Bad Documentation

I advise any museum starting with disorganized collection records to turn to a computer. After the initial start-up, it is easier, quicker, and a lot cheaper to use than any manual system, but it also takes a lot of planning and a large commitment on the part of the museum to carry out the job.[12] See Chapter Eight on computers.

If your museum has a poorly catalogued collection, your first task is to get it into shape. It is difficult to tell someone how to do this without actually seeing the collection, but there are some things that can be done with any collection.

Assemble All the Records

The first task is to assemble all the records you have and try to sort them out. Think of yourself as an auditor with a terrible bookkeeping system that has to be straightened out, particularly as the IRS is on its way. If you only sort the records you have by year, you will have a good start. Try to match correspondence related to your collection with objects listed in your files. If anyone was around when the mess was created, try to get them to advise you. Ask anyone who is familiar with the museum what they know about the collection. Look at old board minutes. Write letters to people who have moved. Just remember the old system made sense to someone at some time; try to figure out their reasoning, no matter how disorganized that may be, and you have won half the battle.

Make a Register

The written information must be in some usable form. I suggest making a register of the old records by accession number (see Figure 1). When you find an accession number, this will quickly lead you to the right data. If there are catalogue cards you can arrange them by the title of the object. That will give you two ways to find something; either by number or title. Computer records can be indexed into some useful form.

Don't Move Anything

Do not move any objects until you have their present locations firmly fixed in the records and in your mind. Objects are often left in one location in the museum for long periods of time, even decades. The relationship of the object to its location may be preserved in the records or the memory of someone associated with the museum.

Make an Inventory

It is a good idea to make an inventory of the museum before you move anything. Do one room at a time, making a short description of *everything* in the room. All objects found in the museum when the new registration system is set up should be noted. If the objects have numbers, make a register of them. A video tape is one way to record the locations of objects before inventory.

In many respects a computer file is a lot easier to use than a card file. For instance, you can search for all the tables about 45 inches long and have a chance of finding the one you are looking at. On the other hand, you will have to be inventive as the computer in a simple search may not be able to find a library table mislabeled as a dining table, and measurements can be inaccurate. The computer can generate a catalogue by number, title, and location if the information exists. These are very useful in inventories.

After you have fixed the location of each object, try to put all of one type of object together, even if only mentally. If you have all the tables together, a description such as "one old table" may suddenly have meaning.[13]

If the Collection Is Numbered

If the collection is numbered, try to reconcile that with the records. The logic of the system will become clearer when you do this. I have found that in these situations, the numbers on the objects usually bear a reasonable relationship to the

OLD BARRACKS MUSEUM
Collections Register

Year ___ 1956 ___

Number	Object	Source	Comment	L	C	I	Location
56.1 A	RUG	MRS ELIZABETH CASE	ORIENTAL, SMALL	✓			COL STOR
56.1 B	"	"	"	✓			COL STOR
56.1 C	"	"	"	✓			COL STOR
56.1 D	"	"	"	✓			COL STOR
56.1 E	"	"	"				
56.1 F	"	"	"	✓			COL STOR
56.1 G	"	"	"	✓			COL STOR
56.1 H	"	"	"	✓			COL STOR
56.1 J	"	"	"	✓			
56.1 K	"	"	"				
56.2 A	MEDALLION WAX, GW	EST. ALBERT ATTERBURY		✓			BOX 93
56.2 B	GUN, MARKET	"		✓			COL STOR
56.2 C	SUNDIAL + PEDESTAL	"		✓			
56.2 D	ENGRAVING, POL I	"		✓			
56.2 E	PHOTOGRAPHS "HERMITAGE"	"		✓			
56.2 F	PORTRAIT GW	"		✓			
56.2 G	" DR WILLIAMS BRYANT	"		✓			
56.2 H	ENGRAVING, SCENES OF CT	"	BY TURNBULL	✓			
56.2 I	A. LINCOLN	"		✓			
56.2 J	BROADSIDE, MASS	"		✓			BOX 105
56.2 K	SETTEE	"	WINDSOR	✓			COL STOR
56.2 L	ENGRAVING, JOHN	"		✓			
56.2 M	WAISTCOAT	"		✓			BOX 32
56.2 N	TABLE, TILT TOP	"	MAPLE	✓			
56.2 "O"	CHAIR, FEATHERED SPLAT	"	SHERATON	✓			
56.2 P	WAIST (DRESS?)	"	EMPIRE	✓			
56.3 A	LEDGER	GERALD PIDCOCK		✓			BOX 167
56.3 B	"	"		✓			BOX 167
56.4	CHAIR LADDERBACK	O.D. OLIPHANT		✓			COL STOR
56.5	SECRETARY	PURCHASE OBA		✓			DEACC.
56.20(?)	SIDE CHAIR	EST. ALBERT ATTERBURY	SHERATON				

Figure 1. A page from an inventory of an incompletely catalogued collection. This register was prepared from paper records before a computer data bank was created, so we would start with a complete record. This list was then compared against the collection. Numbers were entered as they were found. Notice the big gap between 56.7 and 56.20. This is common in collections where a register is not used. Notice that a great number of objects were not found. In actual practice, very few of these objects were actually missing, but most represent inconsistencies in the records.

numbers in the records. And I have found it easiest to make a register of the numbers from the records and check these off as I find the objects. That way I avoid duplications. You will also find numbered objects that bear no apparent relationship to the records.

If the numbering system is completely disorganized, you may have to use a combination of techniques dealing with both numbered and unnumbered collections.

Don't assume that just because the object is marked with an accession number it has been accessioned. Conversely, even if the object is not numbered, it may still have been accessioned.

If the Collection Is Not Numbered

If the collection is not numbered, you will have to assign numbers during the inventory. It is difficult to advise anyone on how this is to be done without seeing the collection records, but these rules apply to almost all situations. You should take steps to see that:

1. The fact the objects are not numbered should be preserved in the numbering system.
   a. If the objects have a known status (i.e., a known provenance or source), you would assign numbers to objects in the same fashion you would for any other accession.
   b. If the objects are of unknown provenance, you accession them as one big group.
      (1). You can assign an artificial year of accession. If you are working in 1996 all the items of unknown provenance are accessioned as if in the year 1995. That is, any object numbered 94.XX.XX is of unknown provenance. If the previous year has been used in your registration system, use system (2).

or;

      (2). You can assign an artificial donor or source number, perhaps the number 1 (one). With this system, if you are working in 1996, all the accession numbers 96.1.XX are of unknown provenance. This is the method I prefer to use instead of an artificial year.
2. You must keep a very accurate register of what you have done.
3. You must place the accession number on each object as it is accessioned.

How to Reconcile the Completed Catalogue

You will end up with three classes of objects:

1. Objects that can be related to the records.
2. Objects that cannot be identified from the records.
3. Records that are not related to any object.

The tendency is to assume that unidentified objects do not have records, and that the loose records refer to missing or stolen objects. Before these assumptions are made, carefully try to match the records with the objects. My experience has been that many of the objects thought to be "missing" actually exist in the collection, but that the records are too disorganized to identify them. Some pretty strange descriptions creep into the files. I have seen measurements off by as much as a foot, beds described as stands, cider presses described as lard presses, and so on. After you have carefully compared the records with the objects, you will have to admit that some discrepancies have crept into your records. These discrepancies can be "resolved" by reaccessioning the objects.

Never Throw Out Old Records

Never throw out old records, no matter how confused they are. Even if the records are completely disorganized, someone in the future may want some information from them. Never discard the old numbering system. Even if you renumber everything, you should carefully note the old numbers in the new records. The old numbers may be referred to in your registration documents.

If There Are No Records

If there are no records, you must treat the collection as a single accession. You can use the same techniques as you would in an unnumbered collection.

Be Complete and Consistent

Often, the reason the old registration methods may be a mess is that whoever was keeping them was not consistent and did not complete what they set out to do. If you do not want someone to curse the day you were born, you must complete what you start and you must be consistent. That means you must account for every object and reconcile all problems in the records. It is better to do one section of the old collection at a time, and do it well, than to try to do it all and be unable to complete what you start. Even if you are not using the most efficient procedures your consistency and completeness will make the system useful.

Deaccessions

There is a rule in treating objects found in the collection: If they are not accessioned and you intend to dispose of them, then you do not need to deaccession them. It saves a lot of steps if you do not accession unknowns just to deaccession them. Disposal is much easier. It is mandatory, however, to make a list of these objects and to get board approval when you dispose of them, so there is some record. You must also be very sure that these objects belong to you and are yours to dispose of.

Be Cautious about Reaccessioning

And finally, if you have a problem, reaccessioning is not always the way to solve it. You can end up with several registration systems. It is better to salvage the old system for in that way you preserve much of the original character of your records. A good way to salvage the old system is to catalogue it. See Chapter Six.

Make a Record of What You Have Done

Write down an exact description of what you have done and make sure this gets preserved in your records. I would recommend binding it in the front of the accession ledger for the years you updated the records, or placing it in your procedural manual.

What you are trying to do is make sure that those who come after you understand what you did and why. It is too much to expect someone to understand the basic logic of your actions without some explanation. I have seen dozens of collections where someone "renumbered" or "recatalogued" it in some illogical and incomplete fashion, leaving no record of what they did or why, and creating a tremendous mess that causes problems for interminable periods of time. If they had left a short explanation, it would have made things easier on the rest of us.

Volunteers and Registration

Museum professionals differ about using volunteers in general, and using them in registration in particular. There is some negative feeling, and volunteers tend to be used mainly in the areas of interpretation and program. Volunteers can be very useful in the area of registration if the professional staff gives some training, sets realistic, specific goals, and works with the volunteers.

Collectors and knowledgeable people might be willing to catalogue your collection in their area of interest. Bottle collectors might work with your bottle collection, stamp collectors with your stamps, gun collectors with your weapons, and so on. If you can tap that source of expertise, you can tap a whole community of interest that can help the museum with exhibits, publications, and collections, who can also steer valuable items into your collection. The computer is ubiquitous in our society, and many people have sophisticated backgrounds in computers and can give you real assistance.

I, personally, find that volunteers are very useful, their knowledge helpful, and their enthusiasm rewarding. I would not run a museum of any size without them.[14]

Ethics
Morals are private but ethics are public

A friend with legal training once advised me never to do anything, no matter how innocent, that I would not mind discussing in open court. For ethics, that is a good rule to follow. Ethics codes usually urge people to avoid even the appearance of impropriety, and the museum collection is one area where that is a sound practice. After January 1, 1997, the Accreditation Commission is going to insist that all museums being accredited adopt an institutional code of ethics. Whether you intend to be accredited or not, it is a good idea to have one.

The museum field has evolved a consensus on ethics and has developed a number of ethics codes.[15] The board ought to formulate such a code considering several factors discussed here. A statement about ethics appears in the sample collection policies in the appendix.

It is not a good idea for the board member or the staff to be in the actual business of privately collecting, buying, and selling in the same area in which the museum's collection falls. These people in posts of trust or honor should avoid going into competition with the museum.[16] People interested in the museum, and curators trained in its field of interest, will, as a matter of course, be knowledgeable about areas similar to that of the museum's collection and may privately own objects which could be in that collection. They may buy and sell from their own collection from time to time. They should inform the board if they have substantial holdings.

If an object that should be in the museum's collection is offered to one of these persons, the person should offer the museum first refusal. If one of these privileged persons sells some of their own collection, they should offer it to the museum first. As a practical matter, the small museum will seldom be in a position to buy one of these objects, but knowledge of the transaction keeps everything visible so the board can be informed and make judgments wisely.

When a museums sells a deaccessioned item, it is best to do this at public auction, rather than private sale. This keeps things in the public eye. Private sales may give the perception of favoritism and self-dealing, serious ethical charges.

It is desirable for a curator to have knowledge of the marketplace. Many great collections have been built by a collaboration between a curator and dealers. On the other hand, it is undesirable for the curator or board member to operate an antique shop or to be a partner, silent or otherwise, in one or to have a similar conflict of interests. I personally do not collect in the same area as the museum at which I work, but it may be desirable for other curators and board members to do so. If there is a potential conflict, the board should set up a mechanism where everything is out in the open, so neither party is injured, but under which both can operate.

At a board meeting, a colleague of mine once had to discuss the price she expected to pay for an object to be auctioned in front of a board member who was going to bid against the museum! You do not want to be in that situation.

Conclusion

The first steps, then, are important. The museum should decide that it is going to have a good registration system and set out to do what is necessary to achieve it.

It is as important to:

- Know why you are doing something as it is to know how to do it.
- Stay within definite boundaries.
- Be consistent and to complete each process before going on to the next step.
- Obtain all the information you can on each object and file it where it can be found.

That sounds like a lot to do, but the consequences of not doing it will take more time than doing everything on this list well.

NOTES

1. I once heard Milo M. Quaife use this analogy at a meeting in Michigan in the 1950s. The exact place and time escape my memory, but it is a good analogy to remember.

2. Although a volunteer-run museum may technically not be accreditable, that does not mean it cannot be well run.

3. AAM, *Museum Accreditation: A Handbook for the Institution* (Washington, DC: AAM, 1990), p. 26. There are provisions in the accreditation process to accredit museums that do not have collections; Marie C. Malaro, *Legal Primer on Managing Museum Collections* (Washington, DC: Smithsonian Institution Press, 1985), pp. 3–18; Malaro offers a lot of practical advice and is the best legal guide for laymen; For an interesting discussion of the definition of the term "museum," see Ramon S. August, "Museums: A Legal Definition,"

Curator, 26, 2 (June 1983), pp. 137–153; Marilyn E. Phelan, *Museums and the Law: A Guide for Officers, Directors and Counsel* (Evanston, IL: Kalos Kapp Press, 1994), pp. 1–2. Phelan is more a book for lawyers than museum people, but if you want a legal definition, you've got it.

4. Pat Nauert, comp., "Glossary," in Dorothy H. Dudley and Irma B. Wilkinson, et al., *Museum Registration Methods* (Washington, DC: AAM, 1979), pp. 409–416; AAM, "Museum Positions: Duties and Responsibilities," *Museum News,* 57, 2 (November/December 1978), pp. 25–26.

5. The Accreditation Commission defines accessioning as, ". . . the creation of an immediate, brief and permanent record utilizing a control number for an object or a group of objects added to the collection from the same source at the same time, and for which the museums has custody, right, or title. Customarily, an accession record includes among other data the accession number, date and nature of acquisition (gift, excavation, purchase, bequest, etc.), source, brief identification and description, condition, provenance, value, and name of staff member recording the accession."

6. The Accreditation Commission defines cataloguing as, ". . . the creation of a full record in complete descriptive detail of all information about an object, assembly, or lot, cross-referenced to other records or files, and often containing a photograph or sketch. Catalog data are usually in the form of cards, sheets, or automated data."

7. Jeanette Toohey, "The Quandary: What is a Curator?" in the "Professionally Speaking" column, MAAM *Courier,* 13, 6 (November/December 1993), p. 4. She thinks the curator is responsible for helping to carry out the museum's mission as well as care for the collection and should be in any planning process.

8. Mary Case, ed., *Registrars on Record: Essays on Museum Collections Management,* Registrars Committee (Washington, DC: AAM, 1988); the role of a registrar was the subject of the first issue of *Registrar's Report* (now *Registrar*), 1, 1, (May 1977), pp. 1–15, which includes an interview with Irma B. Wilkinson; in "Profiles: Janice Dockery," *Registrar,* 10, 1 (Summer/Fall 1993), pp. 15–35, tries to explain what it is to be the registrar of a historical collection.

9. Hedy A. Hartman and Suzanne B. Schell, "Institutional Master Planning for Historical Organizations and Museums," *AASLH Technical Report #11* (Nashville: American Association for State and Local History [AASLH], 1986).

10. There are numerous discussions of collection policies. The best is Marie C. Malaro, *Primer,* pp. 43–51, and *passim*; a useful outline of Malaro's ideas appears in "Collections Management Policies," Anne Fahy, ed., *Collections Management,* Leicester Readers in Museum Studies (New York: Routledge, 1995), pp. 11–28 with a sample collection policy; Daniel R. Porter, III, *AASLH Technical Report #1*; and "Current Thoughts on Collection Policy: Producing the Essential Document for Administering Your Collection," *AASLH Technical Report #7* (Nashville: AASLH, 1985); also Daniel R. Porter, III, "Developing a Collections Management Manual," *AASLH Technical Report #7* (Nashville: AASLH, 1986); Anita Manning, "Self Study: How One Museum Got a Handle on Collections Management,"

Museum News, 65, 6 (August 1987), pp. 61–67; Arminta Neal, Kristine Hagland, and Elizabeth Webb, "Evolving a Collection Manual," *Museum News*, 56, 3 (January/February 1978), pp. 26–30 is more for a science museum but is very useful as to method; the article also appears in Fahy, *op. cit.*; less useful is Marilyn Phelan, *Museums and the Law*, Museum Management Series, Vol. 1 (Nashville: AASLH, 1982), pp. 94ff and *passim*; Dudley and Wilkinson, *passim*, shows policy being handled as a practical matter.

11. The use of a collection committee is not a standard practice in the history museum field, but, in my opinion, it should be. See especially Malaro, *Primer*, pp. 43–51; Allen Ulberg and Patricia Ulberg, *Museum Trusteeship* (Washington, DC: American Association of Museums, 1981); and Brian O'Connel, *The Board Members Book: Making a Difference in Voluntary Organizations* (n.p.: The Foundations Center, 1985).

12. This section was delivered as an address before a session of the MAAM meeting in Washington, DC, 1994; Caroline M. Stuckert, *Cataloging from Scratch: A Manual for Cataloging Undocumented Collections in Small Museums* (n.p.: Caroline M. Stuckert, 1987), is very useful, especially for working with disorganized collections..

13. Dennis R. Pullen, "Inventorying Historical Collections in the Small Museum," *Curator*, 28, 4 (December 1985), pp. 271–285.

14. Daniel B Reibel, "The Use of Volunteers in Museums and Historical Societies," *Curator*, 17, 1 (April 1974), pp. 16–26.

15. Considering that ethical questions come up only occasionally in a typical museum, they have been covered in numerous monographs. See particularly Marie Malaro, *Museum Governance: Mission, Ethics, Policy* (Washington, DC: Smithsonian Institution Press, 1994), *passim*; Robert R. MacDonald, "A Question of Ethics," *Curator*, 31, 1 (1994), pp. 6–9; the AAM, *Code of Ethics for Museums* (Washington, DC: AAM, 1994) has been widely adopted by the museum field; the *AASLH Statement of Professional Ethics* (1996), is essentially the same as the AAM code but is more specific on collections and is more suited to history museums; AAM, "Code of Ethics for Museum Workers," *Museum News*, 52, 9 (June 1974), pp. 26–28, this is the original 1925 code; Stephen W. Weil, *Beauty and the Beasts: Art, The Law, and the Market* (Washington, DC: Smithsonian Institution Press, 1983), pp. 103–190 and *passim*; *ICOM Code of Professional Ethics* (Paris: ICOM, 1987); Patricia Ullberg, "What Happened in Greenville: The Need for Codes of Ethics," *Museum News*, 60, 2 (November/December 1981), pp. 26–29; Association of Art Museum Directors, *Professional Practices in Art Museums, Report to the Professional Practices Committee* (New York: Association of Art Museum Directors, 1971), has had a profound effect on other ethics codes in museums. All the ethics codes in circulation at the time are discussed in AAM, "Ethics Codes, Past, Present and Future," *Museum News*, 67, 2 (November/December 1988), p. 35. The quotation that begins this section was given at a symposium on museum ethics presented by the New Jersey Council of Museums in Morristown, 1986.

16. G. R. Cook, "Should Curators Collect? Some Considerations for a Code of Ethics," *Curator*, 28, 3 (September 1982), pp. 161–171; Joan Lester, "A Code of Ethics for Curators," *Museum News*, 61, 1 (February 1983), pp. 36–40; Cordelia Rose [Introduction], "A Code of Ethics for Registrars," *Museum News*, 63, 3 (February 1985), pp. 42–46; Allen D. Ulberg and

Robert C. Lind, "Personal Collecting: Proceed with Caution," *Museum News*, 69, 5 (September/October 1990), pp. 33–35.

Two

Acquisition

The first stage of the registration process is the acquisition of the object. This process starts with the first contact. Someone may approach the museum with an item they wish to donate or sell, or the museum may approach them. Museums acquire objects mainly by two methods, as gifts and as purchases, but other methods include exchange, bequest, transfer, and collection in the field. Any documents created by this contact, particularly letters, bills of sale, and notes, become the first items in your accession file.[1]

Acquiring Title

The most important thing about these first steps in the registration process is that the museum gets actual title and possession of the object and a document proving that the museum owns it. You would be amazed at the number of museums that cannot prove they own their collections. Title passes to you when you acquire all the rights of ownership, that is the right to do anything that the museum wants to do to the object.

In order to pass good title to you, the person transferring the object must have good title themselves. They must have an unrestricted right to the object and be free to give or sell it to the museum. The museum should question the owner about that right. There is considerable difference between buying an object that has been in a family for generations and buying it from some unknown dealer off the back of a truck.

In the case of gifts, the museums should make sure that there is not some other person in the family with an interest in the object. You cannot acquire an object from a juvenile without parental permission, and even this may come into question when the juvenile reaches majority. With gifts, the first steps that the museum takes should ensure that it acquires these rights:

- The right to display or not display the object as the museum pleases. If the museum is bound to display something permanently, that would bind them to one kind of exhibit forever.
- The right to break up collections. If the museum is given a collection of household objects, it might be expedient to store the glassware in one place and the ceramics in another, rather than keeping it all together. The museum may wish to keep only part of the collection and dispose of the rest.
- The right to dispose of the object as the museum sees fit. Although the museum does not intend to dispose of any of its collection, there are times when it has too many of one thing. They may wish to trade or sell a part of their collection and should not be restricted from doing so.

It is better to acquire all these rights at the beginning and not have to worry about them later.

These rights of property may sound harsh to prospective donors, but donors themselves would not want to own property with any restrictions on it, and neither does the museum. Contrary to what these rights imply, the museum is under a heavy responsibility to keep everything it acquires. Museums that "churn" their collections inevitably get into trouble.[2]

Keep in mind that certain rights may not belong to the owner. The most ordinary ones would be copyrights or trademarks. You can pretty much assume that if the copyright is not specifically transferred to you in writing you do not own it. The law on copyrights is very complex. Copyright notices may not appear on objects dated after January 1, 1978. Trademarks expire periodically, but some are kept alive long after the company that owned them has gone out of business.[3]

It is simpler to acquire the necessary rights with things you buy, but not so simple with gifts.

Purchases

When a museum purchases something, it gets a bill of sale. If there is a willing seller who has unobstructed title to the object, a willing buyer, an exchange of equal value, and all the other processes of the marketplace, then you almost always have a clear title to the object.[4] The bill of sale and all other documents of the transaction should be marked with the accession number of the object and placed in the accession file.

Even the smallest museum needs legal advice on exactly how such purchases should be handled. It is a good idea to have the museum's whole collection policy looked over by a good lawyer.

Gifts

Most museums of any size depend on gifts of objects to make up their collections. When someone gives an object to the museum and the transaction is without value received, but only for good will, the museum's title to the object is not as clear as it is for a purchase. A gift normally passes absolute ownership from the giver to the recipient only when there is the intention to make the gift and free will on the part of the giver—something they, or their heirs, can deny later.

To help establish their title to gifts, museums should have donors sign a "Transfer-of-Title Form" or "Gift Agreement Form." The gift agreement is pretty clear evidence of free will and the intention to make a gift.[5] Actual donors will seldom, if ever, claim their property back. That has never happened to me in thirty-nine years in the museum business, although I know where it has happened at other museums. In these cases, incidentally, the museums refused to return the objects and were upheld. Never, ever, accept a gift without a properly executed gift agreement form. In the absence of any preliminary documents, that will be the first document in the museum's accession file on that particular accession. Such a form should clearly state that the donor is giving up all rights and title to the object. A statement on such a document might be:

Certificate of Gift

By these present I (we) irrevocably and unconditionally give, transfer, and assign to the Hero County Historical Society by way of gift, all right, title, and interests (including all copyright, trademark, and related interests) in, to and associated with the object(s) described below. I (we) affirm that I (we) own said object(s) and that to the best of my (our) knowledge I (we) have good and complete right, title and interests (including all transferred copyright, trademark and related interests) to give.

(Note: If the copyright or trademark is not transferred that has to be noted.[6])

The transfer-of-title should clearly state what is being given, show the date of the transaction, and provide a place for the signatures of the donor and a representative of the museum. In some states you may need a witness to the signature. With this statement, the description of the property, and all the signatures, you have a good claim to the object, but the title may not be absolute, and the watchful museum professional keeps that in mind.

A gift of an object to a museum collection places an obligation on the museum. The obligation is to preserve the object and to keep all historic associations. Although these obligations are seldom mentioned or placed in writing, they are usually assumed by the donor—"You're a museum, after all." Donors and communities become very upset when the museum does not live up to them. In several court cases, museums have been held remiss for failing to perform these unwritten obligations. That places a heavier load on gifts than on purchases, although this rule applies to the whole collection.

If the donor gives you money to buy something, the object purchased is a gift. You still have to get a bill of sale or a receipt for the purchase, but the accession is actually a gift. Because the donor gave you money, the object is much more clearly the property of the museum than the gift of the object itself might be, but objects purchased in this way should be treated as any other gift. Since you already have a document transferring the object, you may not need a gift agreement form, but you should have some document from the donor indicating the gift.

With bequests to the museum, the executor or lawyer handling the estate will usually supply a document such as a copy of a portion of the will or something similar. In many cases, he or she will only produce a letter stating that he or she is executing the will and has the power to transfer the property to the museum. These documents are usually sufficient to establish title to the object and you will not need a gift agreement signed, but every time this comes up check with your lawyers.

Occasionally, you will be bequeathed items with restrictions on them. These restrictions might include the way the bequest is to be acknowledged ("In Memory of B. Knott Forgotten"), but also might include the donation of objects you do not want or restrictions on the bequest, such as requiring that it be kept together in a collection or permanently exhibited. Each instance must be handled individually, but the institution must be careful not to place itself in the position of not being able to break up collections or of always having to exhibit some particular object. You are not in a position to negotiate with the donor. If you accept the object from a bequest, you may have to keep it permanently, unlike other portions of your collections. In these cases, your lawyer can advise you.

Sometimes heirs to an estate will give items in memory of the deceased. These are not bequests from the estate, but are gifts from the heirs, and have to be treated like any other gift.

Museums also acquire objects by law. Objects are turned over to the museum in the normal legislative process. One example would be the Hero County Civil War battle flags being turned over to the Hero County Historical Society by action of the county commissioners. Some objects, such as archives, are sometimes turned over automatically by law. It would be a good idea, mandatory, as a matter of fact, to get a signed letter of transmittal for such a gift. A receipt may be good enough here, but you can never get enough legal advice, so ask your lawyer.

There are "collections in the field." This term usually applies to archaeological and scientific collections, but history museums also acquire objects in this fashion. Salvaging something from a junk pile might be the closest analogy to scientific field collection. If you get to salvage machinery from a factory that is to be torn down, that, too, is collection in the field. You should have some document showing you had the right to do this and that the items collected are yours. Collections in the field are handled as any other accession.

Museums exchange objects with other museums and institutions, or give and receive transfers of objects. These deals are usually done on a friendly basis, but, again, you should have a document showing you have title. In the absence of any other document, the transfer-of-title form should be sufficient documentation. Transfers and exchanges are handled as any other accession or deaccession.

It is not a good idea to accept an object on loan pending its donation as a gift. Some flexibility may have to be exercised here, as the museum may wish to examine it before accepting it or the authorizing person may not be available. There is a method of doing this that is often called by the clumsy title "deposit loan." A deposit loan is a short-term loan (usually less than thirty days) that the museum takes in under much lower standards of care, than other loans. The museum usually does not agree to any responsibility, other than to guard against gross negligence, and places all the responsibility for the delivery and pickup on the lender. These loans have to be tracked very carefully, and cleared as early as possible. Deposit loans are discussed further in Chapter Seven.

Possession of the Object

Warning flags should go up whenever the owner does not want to give possession. Title to the object, and possession of it, are two different things at law, but for practical purposes, you may assume that you do not have title unless you also have possession. In the case of gifts, title passes only with possession, particularly when there is a tax consideration. It would be difficult to imagine a valid purchase without the museum acquiring possession. Occasionally, however, there are situations where possession of an object does not immediately pass to the museum. These deals should not be consummated without the advice of a lawyer and a discussion with the board.

There are "partial" gifts where the museum shares ownership with another museum or person. In these cases, the museum only owns a certain percentage of the object and only has possession a portion of the time. Partial gifts are very difficult to handle. The number of potential problems is infinite. To have a partial gift in storage is ridiculous, and I recommend not accepting a partial gift unless it is an object you just have to have and one that will add significantly to your exhibits.[7]

There are gifts where the owner may retain certain rights. An example would be a famous person retaining the right of publication of his or her papers. This is something to approach carefully, but if you must accept an object with this kind of restriction, put a time limit on it. The life of the donor plus ten to twenty-five years is reasonable.

A museum has to be careful about giving "life tenure" or long-term possession to the donor on objects in the collection. This is particularly true when a tax deduction is involved. The donor usually cannot claim tax deductions unless the title to the property has been transferred and the object itself is in the possession of the museum. You may have trouble getting such property away from the heirs. Museums are rarely able to engage in long and expensive lawsuits. The original owner seems to live forever.

At this point, whether it was a purchase or a gift, the object is now in the possession of the museum and you have title to it. If you do not, go back to "Go" and start again.

Acknowledgment of Gifts

It is an excellent idea to acknowledge all gifts, both privately and publicly. There are several ways to do this. Many organizations have a printed form that they send to the donor to acknowledge a gift. That is adequate, but I prefer a personal letter. A gift is a declaration of faith in the museum and deserves more than a form letter. It takes very little effort to make each one personal. See Figure 2 for an example.

The person who receives this letter will know you really appreciated the gift. Notice the accession number on the lower left. A copy of this letter and of Mrs. Donor's letter of inquiry asking the museum if wants the collection are placed in the accession file. All of these documents, along with the public display of the objects as gifts, may prove the museum's claim to title in the future if the heirs should claim that auntie didn't know what she was doing when she gave away the spoons.

A good place to acknowledge a gift publicly is in your newsletter (see Figure 3). It will give good publicity among people most interested in the museum and will encourage them, too, to give. Another place is a new accessions exhibit in some good corner of the museum. This will be seen by the casual visitor.

If the item is exhibited, the label should acknowledge it as "Gift of Mrs. Deductible Item," or, in the case of a fund, "Purchased by the Faith, Hope, and Charity Fund." This is important, and the donors, their family, and friends will receive a great deal of satisfaction from seeing the name on the label. If the name is left off, the donor and potential donors may quite rightfully might think that you do not care. That is public evidence that the object was a gift. Publication of gifts in your newsletter is also a public announcement of the gift. All this publicity of the object as a gift helps document the museum's claim to it. Courts have ruled that the public display of an object with the unchallenged statement that it is a gift is evidence of the donation.

Some donors don't want their name used publicly. There are various reasons for this, but usually the donor doesn't want the public to know they owned such an object. They fear becoming targets for thieves or ungrateful relatives. You should honor this request when asked. Privacy laws limit the publication of a donor's name to legitimate museum functions such as exhibits or publication of catalogues.

THE HERO COUNTY HISTORICAL SOCIETY, INC.
John A. Hero Mansion
804 East Lincoln Avenue
Hero, Franklin 20123

February 21, 1999

Mrs. B. Generous Donor
26339 York Road
Hero, Franklin 21123

Dear Mrs. Donor:

I wish to thank you for the gift of the 144 commemorative teaspoons. As you know, the Hero County Museum has a large collection of souvenir objects and this gift will greatly enhance this collection. We are planning an exhibit for next year based on this collection and some of your spoons will be an important part of this exhibit. We are placing some of your spoons on display in our "Collectors' Corner" in June.

I wish to thank you not only on behalf of the Museum, but also on behalf of the Board of Directors of the Hero County Historical Society.

Sincerely,

P. Bismarck Adams,
Director

99.12

Figure 2. Thank you letter.

Accessioned Donations

April 1 - August 3, 1995

George Akel: lifeboat oar from the Liberty ship *Ambrose E. Burnside*, 1945.

Margaret M. Baham: hats & clothing worn by her aunt, Ethel Bernard, 1920s-40s.

Brenda Bailey: stereo console & 45 RPM records, 1970.

H.P. Bell: scuppernong wine made & bottled in Pender Co., 1993.

BMS Architects: 6 bottles unearthed on site of former Chamber of Commerce building, early 1900s.

Bladen Lake State Park: 4 turpentine pans used to collect rosin, 1940s.

Charles H. Boney, Jr.: ferry station blueprint, 1920s-30s.

Leslie N. Boney, Jr.: Azalea Festival poster (Bellamy Mansion), 1991.

Sylvia Bowles: sign, doctor's bag & medications from Dr. Daniel C. Roane, 1940s.

Helen K. Chandler: 2 lamp post lamps from garage at 711 Market St., c. 1900-10.

City of Wilmington: newspaper supplement on downtown Wilmington revitalization, 6/16/65.

Nancy Faye Craig: prom dress, crinoline, gloves, shawl, sash, apron & photo, 1961-62.

Sam Daniluk: portable typewriter "Hermes baby featherweight" & cleaning supplies, 1945.

Mrs. M.M. Dunn: newspapers, articles & clippings about the Azalea Festival & local historic sites, 1960s.

Evelyn R. Foster: postcards: Carolina Apts., 1909; Odd Fellows Temple, 1911; Lumina, 1912.

Douglas A. Fox: postcards of historic Wilmington, Wrightsville & Carolina beaches, 1940-50.

Jack F. Hart, Jr.: hammer & hatchet from construction of Dow Chemical plant, 1933.

Lillian Kersh: boating & water safety manuals, 1975-1986.

Edna Williams Mason: James Walker Hospital nurse's uniform, 1950-51.

Norman H. Melton: fossils from horse, crocodile & buffalo of the Lower Cape Fear.

Ann S. Mincy: rifle & bayonet, Japanese Army, 1945; tools used by T.N. Simmons.

Wanda Moore: photo of Robert Moore, ca. 1975.

NC Azalea Festival: posters, 1992 & 1995.

Glenn Tetterton Opheim: dish towel from Tickhill Estfeld Primary School, Doncaster, England, 1995.

Charlotte J. Parker: programs, magazines & ID pins, 1989-93.

Marilyn Pierce: USAF memorabilia from Leon Pierce, 1941-53; newspaper articles about regional history.

E. L. "Buck" Potter: Stevens .22 caliber rifle, c. 1930; Winchester .32-.40 caliber rifle, c. 1900.

Robert L. Pratt: camera collection, 1899-1962.

Jimmy Savage: men's cologne ampules, 1960s.

Lydia McK. Stokes: US Army tunic, jodhpurs & Sam Browne belt, 1930s.

Doug Swink: Lumina ad, 5/20/46.

Helen Willetts: *Coast/Vacationer's Guide* & Bald Head Island license plate, 1975.

A. Jarvis Wood, Jr.: *The Health Bulletin*, Oct. 1954.

Frances D. Worrell: professional floor model hair dryer, c. 1940.

E.B. & Della W. York: cast-iron cooking/wash pot; unearthed near Currie, NC, 1950.

Image Archives

Robert Cantwell: videotape of Wilmington waterfront fire, 1953.

Barry Faulkner: photos of Hurricane Hazel damage to Carolina Beach, 1954.

Mary M. Gornto: photo of 8 Wilmington businessmen, including W.H. & Alex Sprunt, Thomas R. Orrell in Paris, 1922.

Wayne Jackson: WMFD-TV photos & log sheet for first-day broadcast, c. 1954.

Michelle Matheny: photo of Michael Jordan in Birmingham Barons uniform, 1994.

Mrs. Leslie Silva: photos of Nelson Silva & his Simmons Sea- Skiff, 1987 & 1993.

Annie Talley: photos of 1955 Sea- Skiff.

Kenneth L. Todd: photo of Michael Jordan & Jarrad Taunt, 1982.

Thomas E. Williams, Sr.: photo of Laney HS basketball team w/ Michael Jordan, 1980-81.

Unaccessioned Donations

Jay Barnes: book: *North Carolina's Hurricane History*, 1995.

Nancy Faye Craig: magazines: *American Home*, Mar. & Aug. 1961; *Better Homes & Gardens*, Dec. 1956.

Betty J.B. Deangury: *1938 National Guard of the United States, State of NC* yearbook .

Ray Dew: loblolly pine cookies (cross-section), 1995.

Jack F. Hart, Jr.: photo of Dow Chemical employees near highway historical marker, 1993.

Jack Miller: 5 issues of New York *Times*, 1918-1919.

Susan Morgan: baby's lace jacket; lace & embroidery slip, c. 1910.

Jessie Moseley: nightgown & scarf, c. 1950; book, *Blue Book Speller*, c. 1920.

NC Azalea Festival: Azalea Festival posters, 1992 & 1995.

NC Wildlife Commission: flying squirrel.

NHC Public Library: books: *Indian Wars in North Carolina*, 1963; *Printing in North Carolina*, 1946.

Julian Tusch: photocopy of newspaper article, "The All New Hanover County Basketball Team", 1981.

USDA: adult female beaver; 2 sub-adult male beavers.

Figure 3. A page from a newsletter showing donations. A single listing like this can establish your ownership of gifts. It is also good public relations, and will stimulate other gifts. Notice that the museum has three types of collections, and makes very sure that their audience knows into which collection the object is going. People donating to the study or education collection are under no illusions that their gift is going to the museum's permanent collection. This is from the Cape Fear Museum (Wilmington, NC) newsletter, *Waves and Currents*, 15, 2 (1995).

Board Action

The board of trustees has the ultimate responsibility for the museum. When the museum accepts an object for its collection, it is also accepting a rather heavy long-term responsibility and that makes it a board matter. The board should have knowledge, if not the actual approval, of the acceptance of each object. That does not necessarily mean that every object has to be taken before the board and discussed. That would tie the board up with minutiae that is best left to the professional staff. The easy way is to have the director take a list of accessions before the collections committee. Once approved, this can be submitted with the committee's report. By accepting the report, the board approves of the accession. This action will give the board necessary oversight without creating undue interference.

On accepting a gift, it should be made clear to the donor that the museum does not expect any problems with acceptance; in fact, it is wise to mention in passing that the committee must approve. If the museum does not want the object, this provision allows them to turn down the object gracefully and spread the blame over the anonymity of a number of people. The acceptance of the collections report should be a routine thing, similar to the secretary's reading of the minutes. The report keeps the board informed, gives them some oversight over the collection, and reminds them of their responsibility.[8]

Properties Are Not Collections

Properties are expendable portable physical assets of the museum, such as desks, chairs, vacuum cleaners, lawn mowers, etc. These are items that will eventually wear out and have to be discarded. Properties are more of a problem for an accountant than a curator. The museum should state in the collection policy that the properties are not collections and they should not be treated as such. This means that properties should not be accessioned and that collection items should not be used as properties.

Many museums use reproductions of objects in their exhibits or for education programs. These reproductions are properties and should not be treated as collections even though you may keep them separate from the other properties. They should definitely not be accessioned.

If a reproduction is made by a well-known artisan, it may have a high aesthetic, monetary, or a cultural value. These objects might best be in the collection. This is a quandary, for if it is in the collection it should not be used in programs. We are going to discuss a tiered collection, where each tier receives different treatment, and that is one solution to the problem of valuable properties.

The Accession File

At this point you have a group of documents associated with the collection. These should be assembled into an accession file. Some museums have a separate file folder on each accession, some on each object, and some have one for the year. The kind you use will depend on the number of documents you have and your ability to store them. In any case, the accession number should be written in soft (#2) pencil on each document, so that it is associated with the object. An accession file will continue to grow as letters and other documents come in, years after the file is set up. This is the permanent record of the museum and should be in a fire-resistant file cabinet, if you can afford one. It is not a bad idea to microfilm the accessions file periodically and to keep the film in a safe place.

What Not to Do and When Not to Do It

I repeat myself here about several things that I have already recommended not be done when acquiring an object. Once more, with feeling:

- Do not accept a gift without a transfer of title or buy an object without a bill of sale.
- Be very careful about accepting a gift that has any restrictions on it.

A major mistake a museum can make in the acquisition process is to put a valuation on the object for tax purposes. It is considered unethical to "buy" a donation with a high or inflated evaluation. It is illegal, too.[9] The museum can protect itself by declaring in the collection policy or registrar's manual that it will not make evaluations. It is the donor's responsibility to get a correct value for the gift for tax purposes. You should be more than willing to cooperate with the donor on getting a professional evaluation and by making the object available to the appraiser if necessary. As part of the gift, the donor may want the museum to pay the appraiser. This is the same, actually, as the museum making the appraisal and it should not be done. You may lose an occasional object by refusing to do this, but you will keep your integrity.

On the other hand, value is often part of the description. You may have two china plates, one of them worth $500 and the other 50¢. Another example would be an object associated with a famous person. The association gives it a value beyond its value as an artifact. An example might be a Civil War uniform. If worn by an anonymous soldier from an unknown locality, it is a specimen. If worn by a local soldier whose history is known, it is a valuable artifact. If you insure your collection, you will usually have to place a value on each object in the collection. This is the "book" value. The book value is often different than the "fair market" value, but the two should not be too far apart. The value should not be public information and should never be discussed with the donor.

To review: The first step in the registration process is the acquisition of the object. The museum must make sure that it actually acquires title to the object, that there are no restrictions on the museum's use of the object, and that all information about the object is recorded.

NOTES

1. There is an extensive discussion of the acquisition process in Malaro, *Primer*, pp. 52ff, on the subject of ownership see particularly pp. 56–69; Franklin Feldman, Stephen E. Weil, and Susan D. Biederman, *Art Law: Rights and Liabilities of Creators and Collectors*, 2 vols. (Boston: Little, Brown & Co., 1986), II, 1ff; Phelan, *Guide*, pp. 273–306.

2. "Churning" consists of acquiring and disposing of objects rapidly.

3. Nicholas D. Ward, "Copyright in Museum Collections: An Overview of Some Problems," *Registrar*, Part 1, 6, 2 (Fall 1989), pp. 13–19, and Part 2, 7, 1 (Spring 1990), pp. 2–11. There is also an article in *ibid.*, 6, 2 by Leonard D. Duboff, "Copyright Law for Photographers," pp. 1–13, which covers the present copyright law in some detail.

4. Malaro, *Primer*, pp. 56–59; Phelan, *Museum Law*, pp. 94f.

5. Phelan, *Museum Law*, p. 99.

6. Reprinted from Marie Malaro, *A Legal Primer on Managing Museum Collections* (Washington, DC: Smithsonian Institution Press, Copyright 1985), p. 137, with their permission. She also shows another form with simpler language.

7. Marsha S. Haines, "Partial Gifts: When Half a Loaf Is Better than None," *Museum News*, 70, 4 (July/August 1991), pp. 68–70.

8. Malaro, *Primer*, p. 13.

9. Phalen, *Museum Law*, p. 106, says that it is not illegal, under certain circumstances, for a museum to evaluate gifts, but then the museum becomes an interested party. Malaro, *Primer*, p. 25, says it is a bad practice and this view echoes the opinion of the museum field.

Three

The Accession Number

The two most important parts of the museum registration system are the registration documents on each object and the object itself. Without some means to tie the particular object to its particular documentation, there is no registration system. The accession number is that means. One of the fascinating things about the registration process is the accession number. One sees those little numbers painted on everything in the museum. As a matter of fact, one had better see one of these numbers on every object in the museum or something is wrong with the system.

Accession numbers will be a lot simpler if you do not think of them as classification numbers but as a serial registration number. The accession number may have some of the characteristics of a part number that not only serially registers each part, and may convey some information about the part as well, but it does not classify it.

To be efficient, any numbering system must be sequential. That is, it must start at a particular point in the series (usually the first available unit, say, 1 [one]), and proceed sequentially number, by number, until the end. Although this may not sound very profound, you would be surprised at the number of systems where this is not true and at the number of problems this causes. To make sure that the numbering system is sequential, an accession register is used. Without a register, it is practically impossible to keep the numbers in some logical order. Registers are discussed in Chapter Four and elsewhere.

The nature of the registration system affects the numbering system you will use. For this reason I am going to use the alternatives available to you in numbering systems and explain the rationale of museum registration. So if you will bear with me, I will spend a great deal of time explaining numbering systems.

The Single-Number System

The easiest system to use is one with a single whole number for each object. The first object is numbered "1" (one), the second "2" (two), *seriatim*. The nine hundred and twelfth object would be "912" and the ten thousandth three hundredth and ninety-eighth would be "10398." Nothing can be simpler than this! In fact, its logical construction and its very simplicity caused it to be used by the early museums in their first attempts to register objects. The Smithsonian Institution and National Park Service uses a modified version of this system to this day. Although it has been replaced, the increasing use of computers for museum registration has caused some people to reevaluate this system.

The system has a lot going for it. The single-number system has no complications. It is easy to understand. One does not have to make decisions but simply take the next available number. This may be important in small museums with inexperienced or untrained staffs and, perhaps, periods with no staff. It also gives you the finite size of the collection.

There are some problems with the single-number system. If you get three accessions at once, of which one has two objects, one has eight, and the third has thirty-two, you have to complete the first accession before going on to the next. This is because your system is strictly sequential and does not easily allow for entering one object of an accession now and another later. If you tried to allow for this by assigning eight digits to the second accession and then went on to the third accession you would have a problem if you suddenly discovered nine objects, or only seven, in the second accession. The third accession of thirty-two objects may be much more important than the others, but you have to wait to do it until you have completed the other two because it is out of sequence. If the collection grows, the numbers may become very large. The donor of the objects is not identified in any particular way except as a block of numbers in a sequence. Museums account for their accessions by year, but there is no particular way to identify accessions by year except, again, as a block of numbers.

For this reason the single-number system has fallen out of favor with museums and has been replaced by other systems that I will discuss below.[1]

The Two-Number System

To resolve some of the problems with the single-number system, museums have adopted a number that I will call the control number. This control is usually the year the accession is made. If the year is 1995, then the control will be "95." The second number is a catalogue number. The first item registered would be 95.1, the second 95.2, the 394th would be 95.394, etc. This system has some advantages. It divides the collections into blocks by year and makes accounting easier. It stops the incessant sequence of one number following another and allows you to deal with groups of objects.

Some museums write this number as XX.95. It is not too important which method you use as long as you are consistent. However, listing the year first makes a long string of numbers more readable. If there is a standard in the method of numbering it would be to list the year first.

The two-number system has all the problems of the single number system except the easy ability to divide the accessions by year. You have to complete each accession before going on to the next, and donors are not identified in any way by the numbering system.

The Three-Number System

Out of these considerations museums have developed what I will call the three-number system (sometimes called the "trinomial system"). In this system the second number is a source number and there is a third number that I will call the catalogue number. This number is added to the two-number system.

In the three-number system, the first number, or control, is usually the year of accession, the second the source number, and the third the number of the object is the accession or the catalogue number. In this example, 95.23.14, "95" represents the year the accession was made; "23" represents the twenty-third accession made in this year; and the "14" represents the fourteenth object in that particular accession. That is, there were thirteen objects registered before this one in the same accession. All objects numbered 95.23.XX come from the same source at the same time. This number may be written 14.23.95 or 23.95.14.

The numbers in the last two examples will not line on a page as well as they will when the year is placed first. That may be the reason that most museums place the year first, the control second, and the catalogue number third.

The main advantages of the three-number system are, first, you do not have to worry about how many objects there are in each accession. The system can take care of any number. I once had over 3,100 objects in one accession. One does not have to take the accessions in sequential order, although you do have to complete them all before the end of the year.

The second advantage, and perhaps the most important, is that it identifies the donor or source of the accession by number. In fact, as we shall see, the three-number system can convey a lot of information depending on how it is structured.[2]

The three-number system resolves most of the problems that plague the other two numbering systems. This is the reason it has been almost universally adopted by history museums in the United States today.

These three systems have withstood the test of time and will fit any museum situation. There is no reason for you to go out and reinvent the wheel and develop your own system when these are perfectly acceptable.

Which System Should You Use?

It is very difficult to advise anyone on which system to use without actually seeing the museum, talking to the people involved, and looking at the rationale of the collection. I suggest considering these factors in selecting the numbering system you should use:

- The single-number system will best fit a small volunteer-run museum with a small collection and no real potential for growth. The system is simple to understand and administer. You can grasp the whole system with a quick glance in the records. If the collection should grow, or circumstances should change, the numbering system can always be changed to one of the other systems.

- The two-number system will best fit a museum where the museum has a small collection and the accessions are infrequent and small in size. An example where this system would be useful would be an art museum that acquires only eight or ten objects in six or eight accessions each year.
- The three-number system should be used in all other situations. This system is flexible and fits a variety of circumstances that come up every year in an active museum collection. The three-number system is standard in the history museum field and is readily understandable to museum professionals.

Contrary to what some people believe, the two-number and three-number systems will easily fit into most computer programs.

Collection Numbers

The control number can convey a lot of information and does not always have to represent the year of acquisition. It can be used to correct an anomaly in the system, as a collection number, or it can indicate a change in collection practices.

Older museums often have separate and distinctly defined collections exist inside the museum collection. Sometimes there is a good reason to separate the collections if only in the registration system. Perhaps the museum was once two separate and distinct institutions that have merged. Perhaps one was a schoolhouse museum and the other a mansion. They each have collections that should be kept apart, at least on paper. One can identify these collections by several means. A collection number is usually a prefix on an existing number. It might look like this:

M65	M32.12	M32.12.3
S65	S32.12	S32.12.3

or

1.65	1.32.12	1.32.12.3
2.65	2.32.12	2.32.12.3

In these examples, the "M" or "1" stands for "mansion" and the "S" or "2" stands for "schoolhouse." With either of these systems you can easily tell an item from one collection from an item from another. The letter version is a little shorter and more understandable, and is favored for that reason.

You have to be careful, for without the collection indicator it will be easy to confuse an object from one collection with an object from the other. For this reason, museums generally avoid collection numbers although, as I shall illustrate, they are very useful in specialized cases.[3]

The collection number does not have to be a prefix but can be indicated by the year or the control number. I list several examples below.

The reason for discussing a collection number at all in a book aimed at small museums is that it is very common to find complete collections of known provenance already existing in the museum collection that, for one reason or another, have to be kept distinct from the rest of the collection. A typical example is a museum that is the successor of a D.A.R museum. There is a requirement that the D.A.R. museum be kept distinct from the successor museum's collection, at least in the records.

Someone gave the museum a collection of stuffed birds in 1910 and a log cabin and its contents in 1933. The museum was given a defunct school system museum in 1956. They completely modernized their registration system in 1962. If you think I am exaggerating, I am describing a collection I once administered (with the exception of the log cabin), along with thirty years of bad record keeping.

It is better to assign a control number than a collection number. In this case, the year of accession is used as the control number. It would be an "artificial" year. All things considered, a control number is a collection number. Using the examples given above, you would assign a separate control number for each collection. If you found these numbers in your collection you would know quite a bit about the object.

9.26.XX (from the D.A.R. museum founded in 1909).
10.26.XX (from the bird collection given in 1910).
33.26.XX (from the log cabin museum given in 1933).
56.26.XX (from the defunct school system museum given in 1956).
61.26.XX (from the museum collection before the modern registration system which was started in 1962, but which does not contain any of the known collections listed above).
[From here on, one would use the year of accession for the year number.]
62.26.XX (from the modern museum registration system adopted in 1962).

This arrangement will work best with the two- or three-number system, which may be one reason for adopting one of these systems. A version of this system can be used with the single-number system, using controls with the earlier collections, and a single number with the new accessions.

Using a Number to Indicate Special Conditions

Another use of special numbering techniques in a registration system is to indicate certain problems with the collection. If you have large numbers of objects that are "unknown" or "found in the collection," a special source number might be a way of indicating them. If you give all unknowns the accession number "1" (one) each year, then they will be readily apparent. A number such as 86.1.34 will tell you that this object is of unknown origin.

We used a system at Old Economy, where the whole collection was of "unknown" origin. It had all been acquired in 1938 but only a partial registration of the collection had been made. There had been some unrecorded acquisitions later. We gave all unknowns the control number "1," except for Harmony Society related items, which were later given the control number "2." Examples would be:

75.1.XX (object of unknown origin found in the collection).
75.2.XX (unknown object of presumed Harmony Society manufacture or use).
75.3.XX (an acquisition that was accessioned using normal practices).

Accounting for unknowns in this fashion does not relieve you from eventually having to get good title to them.

Accession Ledgers

It was common for museums in the 18th, 19th, and early 20th centuries to have accession ledgers. These ledgers are usually bound record books in which the objects are listed in the order of acquisition. The ledgers were a combination of register and accession record. They often contained the name of the object, a brief description, and the name of the donor or source. There is, more often than not, a number assigned to each object. These accession ledgers, if well kept, were considered quite adequate for the time, and can be the basis of a good registration system today. There are large modern museums that are presently still using a form of accession ledger and doing quite well. I recommend using a version of it in the bound accession records. Figure 4 shows a page from a ledger.

Where no number is assigned to the object in the ledger, you should make a working copy of the ledger and number the objects sequentially beginning at the front of the book. As you find objects, you can put the number that belongs on the object. The two- and three-number systems work best in these cases. If a number has been assigned in the ledger, use that number. If there are inconsistencies, you will have to work them out. Be sure not to use the original book, as it is a primary record. Make a copy.

Registers, especially those used to track accession numbers, and ledgers, are discussed in the next chapter.

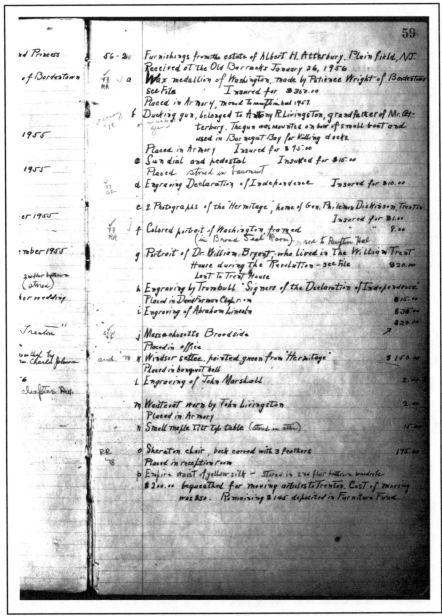

Figure 4. An example of a page from a ledger kept from 1902 to the present. Apparently, originally there were no numbers. Later, a combination of two- and three-number systems were installed with little consistency. Although the information is sketchy, it was the basis for a complete catalogue system.

How to Handle the Centuries

If the museum's collection predates the 20th century, and with the 21st century around the corner, there must be a way to tell one century apart from another. The most common way to handle this is to assign the whole year to the accession number, i.e.,

1786.32.3   1886.32.3   1986.32.3

or

786.32.3   886.32.3   986.32.3

Since many history museums were started in the 20th century, the control number only indicates the unit and digit of the century. In other words, in an accession number such as 89.32.2, the "89" really stands for 1989. The year 2000 is rapidly approaching and one has to allow for it in one's numbering system. In the case of the two-digit control (such as "89"), you place the number 0 (zero) or 20 in front of the control. An accession number from the year 2086 would look like this:

086.32.3 or   2086.32.3

With this system you can easily tell in which century the object was accessioned. A single-number system does not require any adjustment for centuries.

Letters

A lot of people put letters in perfectly good numbering systems. A common sight in collections is something like this:

88.12.2a   Teapot:
88.12.2b   Lid:

This is usually unnecessary. If you have described the teapot accurately, then you will have stated that it has a lid. You hardly need the number 88.12.2b to tell that one object is the teapot and the other is the lid. The same accession number will do for both objects. This rule will apply where the parts of the object are dissimilar but will be permanently associated with each other. In this case, the teapot and its lid are seldom separated.[4]

In sets of objects, such as dining room chairs, you should number each object individually. Although strongly associated with each other, the chairs will not always be kept together. It is confusing to give all the chairs the same number and then label each one separately "a," "b," etc.

An example where letters may be necessary would be a pairs of shoes, stockings, or gloves. These are usually alike and will generally stay together. In this case, it might be a good idea to assign the same accession number and label one stocking "a" and the other "b."

Another problem with letters is that they often get confused with numbers. The rule is, that whenever possible, avoid cluttering up a perfectly good numbering system with a bunch of letters.

A computer can easily make a duplicate record for pairs or sets and this record, given another number, will obviate the necessity for letters at all.

Loan Numbers

The necessity for loan numbers is discussed in Chapter Seven. Whatever system of numbering loans you use, it is important that that you do not confuse your loan numbers with your accession numbers. It is a common practice to reverse the accession number to get a loan number, thus

Accession Number	Loan Number
86.23.2	2.23.86

With this system, however, you will inevitably get the two numbers confused at some point when the year '02 rolls around again. The best method is to place the letter "L" (for "loan") in front of the loan number and change the order you list the numbers; e.g.,

Accession Number	Loan Number
86.23.2	L2.23.86

In the example, the "L2.23.86" is the second object in the 23d loan in the year 1986. There will be less likelihood of confusion using this method. An example of a ledger for loan numbers is shown in the appendix (C-11).

The Difference Between an Accession, Registration, Catalogue, and Classification Number

Some people place a great deal of significance on the number and treat it almost as a mystical thing. The only purpose of the number is to give you a handy method of identifying the object. It's handier than using letters or writing all the data on the object.

There is a number used to tie the object to the records. That number is created and placed on the object when the object is accessioned. That is why the numbers are usually called "accession numbers." When the object is accessioned it has been registered. So this same accession number is also a registration number. Why some museums have two numbers for this purpose is incomprehensible to me.

An object is usually classified in history museums by how it is used. Since the number only ties the object to the record, it cannot properly be called a classification number. Some museums create classification numbers. Classification numbers do not work well in a history museum. For a discussion of this, see particularly the section on lexicons in Chapter Four.

The reason for having a catalogue number vs. an accession number is that the number will classify or identify the object for you by the number alone. It is understandable that you might want to classify all the objects in the museum collection by their number. All the clothing would have one number, all the dresses would have a subclassification under this, and a particular style of dress would have a sub-subclassification, and so on. This has been attempted many times with varying degrees of success. As a matter of fact, you sometimes see collections catalogued with a system in which all tools begin with "T" and all the furniture begins with "F," etc. There are frequently subclassifications such as "TC" standing for carpenters tools. These systems break down almost as soon as they are created.

A term such as "plane, smoothing" shows you exactly where to place the record in the catalogue. Calling a smoothing plane a "TC6" unnecessarily complicates the registration process, ignores the fact that you already have a perfectly good classification system by terminology, and is redundant.

Despite this, some museums have two numbers for each object; an accession number and a catalogue number. I have never understood why. The largest and best-run museums in the country have enough trouble keeping track of one set of numbers, let alone two, and you are no exception to this.[5]

Numbers and Computers

The numbering system used in a museum and the computer come frequently into conflict. The problem is not the entry. You can create a field that will take anything you can create on a keyboard. The problem is to get this to sort in some logical sequence. More and more, computer programs will logically sort accession numbers. There is a solution for those that won't.

If you have a six-figured field (xxxxxx) and put a number in the first field (1xxxxx), many computer programs treat this as the number 100,000 not 1 (one). Letters often do not always sort in any logical sequence, as the lower case "a" may come after 9 (nine) and uppercase letters sort differently than lowercase, etc. This would not be too much of a problem except that the periods, in a number such as 93.87.62, cause the accession number to be sorted as if it were letters.

There are several ways around this. The best method is to look for a program that will handle your numbering system. If you cannot find that, the most common solution is to fill the blanks with zeros. The number 1 (one) will look like this;

00000001

Keep in mind that the leading zeros are used only in the accession record and not on the object.

You can put each element of the number in a separate field, but this only puts the problem into several places instead of one.

More and more computer programs are designed to get around this problem. It is one of the questions you should ask about when buying a program.

Library Classification Numbers

Many people look at a library catalogue and wonder why the same kind of numbering system won't work in a museum. A library classifies a book by its subject and arranges the book alphabetically by author in that classification. The difference between our system and the ones libraries use is that the library number, in most cases, indicates where the book is shelved, something that won't work in a museum.

Actually, we use a similar system based on what the object is called, but without the classification number, since the museum classification has nothing to do with where the object is stored. Some people in the museum field see the library classification number and think it would be perfect if a similar number would do their classification for them. A few systems attempt this. I have seen a collection accessioned with Dewey Decimal Numbers, and it was not badly done, but normally such systems don't work. The museum catalogue is just a device to hold the catalogued list. Our catalogues are classified by broad families of objects with similar uses, and arranged by specific uses inside that. Individual objects are classified by what they are called. An accession number is not a classification number, but just a device to identify a particular object. It is more on the order of a part number.

Other Types of Numbering Systems

The numbering systems I have described work best with history, art, and anthropology museum collections. There are other numbering systems for books, archives, and archaeological specimens. Science museums have several methods that fit their varied collections. When assigning numbers to these specialized collections it is best to use the system common to the discipline. However, if you have a small collection of such objects, it may not pay to set up a separate numbering system for just a few objects. As an example, at Old Economy we accessioned books that were part of the collection, using a standard museum system, and used the Library of Congress system on the reference books.

Conclusion

When beginning or updating a registration system it is important to spend a little time developing the numbering system that sits your situation. The system can make it a lot easier on you later. There is nothing particularly complicated about numbering systems. If they are well thought out, they tend to maintain themselves, once they are in place. They can affect the ease of entering data and accessioning. It is wise to set up a system that fits your needs rather then adopt someone else's system. there is nothing to stop you from adopting a new numbering system as your needs change, although I would caution you against renumbering the whole collection.

NOTES

1. For an excellent discussion of accession numbers, and these problems in particular, see Dudley and Wilkinson, pp. 22–27.

2. A number of my friends feel the three-number system was developed to account for the source of the object, but I believe it was developed to resolve the problems of the other two systems. The problems with the single- and two-number systems would not be as great if you were using only a ledger, but the three-number system works better with cards.

3. A good example of the need for a collection number can be seen in the Pennsylvania Historical and Museum Commission. The PHMC has about sixty separate historic sites and museums, some of which collections are made distinct by law. The PHMC assigns a two-letter code to each site or museum (Old Economy is "OE" and the number would be OE67.23.9). A master number is kept by the registrar, but this does not appear on the object.

4. Sue Hanna, then collections manager of the Pennsylvania Historical and Museum Commission, argued during a presentation on cataloguing at the 1992 MAAM Annual Meeting, that if all parts of the object have letters, then one could tell there was more than one part to the object should the parts be separated.

5. An example of a registration system using catalogue numbers can be seen in Ralph H. Lewis, *Manual for Museums* (Washington, DC: National Park Service, 1979), pp. 150–152. In this example, the Park Service uses a single-number system for its accession number and another single-number system for its catalogue number, which must cause endless confusion when these two sets of numbers inevitably equal each other. Dudley and Wilkinson, p. 410, and *passim*, thinks a catalogue number is for identification, but nowhere in the book is the use of catalogue numbers explained, indicating their low level of acceptance in the museum field.

Four

Accessioning

The second stage of registration is the accessioning process. To accession an object means to take it into the museum's collection. This is a serious step.

Before the object is accessioned it is a piece of property with which the owners can do anything they wish. They can give it to their Uncle Charley, destroy it, paint it green, or put it out in the barn. A property (such as a vacuum cleaner) is a depreciable item whose life is measured by the accounting practices of the museum. Property will eventually be disposed of with very few regrets or complications.

An accession is a different matter. Once an object is accessioned into a museum collection it takes on a whole new life. It becomes something that is protected by law and custom. An accessioned object is meant to be given highly specialized care and kept forever.[1] Disposing of it, called deaccessioning, is a complicated process that takes considerable time and effort and may result in an adverse public controversy.

It is wise, therefore, to have a well thought-out accession policy that is strictly applied. The reason to have a sound accession policy is that it means that you have fewer chances of accessioning objects that you will later have to deaccession. You have to have a sound deaccession policy as well.

The accessioning process consists of making a place for the object in the museum registration system and creating a permanent record of it. The accessioning process consists of the following steps:

1. Acquiring right and title to the object. I have discussed this process in Chapter Two on acquisition.
2. Assigning an accession number. I have discussed this in Chapter Three on numbers.
3. Making a record of the object.
4. Marking the object.

These actions are usually done all at once, but each is a separate process. It is important that the object be accessioned almost immediately after the museum takes possession of it or some of the information that comes with it will be lost.

Creating a Record for the Object

Each object must have a primary record of its existence. This is usually called the "accession record." It is created from the worksheet (see Figure 5). Each of these records should be distinct from all the others. It should follow a format so that the same information is recorded for each object, and that the information is adequate. You can have many problems if you assign more than one accession to a record, have gaps in the sequence, misnumber the object, or do not record enough information. I am not going to detail every problem, but almost all difficulties with records start with poor accession practices.

The Log

Since the number identifies each accession, you must have a method of assigning accession numbers in some logical sequence that will assure that there are no gaps or duplicates. A simple way to control this is to have a log. A log need only be simple stenographer's notebook where each accession is listed with its accession number in the order assigned. These are checked off as the records are created. At the end of the year, the whole log is checked off against the ledger to make sure that all accessions are recorded (see Figure 6).

Hero County Historical Society

Name of Object:	Accession Number:
Classification:	Old Number:
Source: Address:	
Method of Acquisition:	Date:
Special Terms of Acquisition:	
Value: Authority:	Date:
Location:	Date
Physical Condition: Priority:	
Conservation Treatment:	Date:

Description:
Part of a pair or set?   Material(s):
Place of Manufacture: Date:
Artist/Designer/Manufacturer/Distributor:

User(s):   Date:
Place of Use: Date:
Association with Person, Place, or Event:

Association with a Social, Ethnic, etc. Group:

Marking, Inscriptions:
Measurements: W   D   H
Provenance:
Intangibles:
   Style:
   Social Function/Value:
   Other:

Compiler: Authority, if different:
Comments:

This worksheet is an adaptation of fields suggested by the Common Agenda Data Bases Task Force (1989).

Figure 5. Worksheet.

93.1.1	BOOK	LIVES OF SIGNERS
93.1.2	DECORATIVE	TILE
93.1.3	PENCIL SKETCH OF	PAPER MILL
93.1.4	POSTCARD	FOLDER
93.1.5	LITHOGRAPH	, LADY W's RECEPTION
93.1.6	LITHOGRAPH	, B. ROSS
93.1.7	ENGRAVING	, LORD STIRLING
93.1.8	INDENTURE	OBA/STATE NJ
93.1.9	ENGRAVING	WM. PENN
93.1.10	RUG	
93.1.11	WARMER, FOOT	
93.1.12	BOX, CONTRIBUTION	
93.1.13	FLAG	BICENT OF IMAGE.
93.1.14	"	" " "
93.1.15	"	" " "
93.1.16	POSTCARD	NY WORLD'S FAIR 1938
93.1.17	PAMPHLET	" " " "
93.1.18	PHOTOGRAPH	OB
93.1.19	"	"
93.1.20	"	"
93.1.21	"	"
93.1.22	COVERLET -ANN DOUGLASS	
93.1.23	PHOTO	WWI RED CROSS

Figure 6. A page from a log. This simple device keeps your accession numbers in order. It will be useful even with a computer. It is not, however, a permanent record. The permanent record is the register.

A log helps the lone professional, who has many distractions, keep track of the accessions. It is very useful in a museum that has a number of people accessioning objects. It gives the registrar control over the issuing of numbers. A log is useful with either a computer or manual system. It is one of those low-tech things in our hi-tech world that helps keep everything on the right track.

The Register

The log is not a permanent record. You need some permanent and unalterable way of recording the sequence. The device you use is a register. This register can be created in a number of ways.

Manual Systems

With a manual system the register should be in a bound record book that keeps the whole list of accessions for the museum in the proper sequence (see Figure 7). You can have a separate register, or use a ledger, which I will discuss below, in its place. I prefer to keep a separate accession register, but if you can keep good control over the ledger, a separate register is not necessary. See Appendix C-5.

Acc. No.	Objects	Source	Date
999.1	Decorative tile, bicentennial	Wilma Wighter	1/18/99
999.2	Set of chisels	Wall Workman	3/17/99
999.3	Desk, late 19th c	Wand Wonderful	8/23/99
etc.			

Figure 7. A sample of a collections register. It has just enough information to lead you to the right object. Its sole purpose is to keep your accession numbers in order. If you can do this from the ledger, it saves a step.

The purpose of the register is to keep your accessions in order, so it need not carry much information. All that is necessary is the accession number, a brief description of the accession, the source, and the date. Entry into the register should be made at the time the accession is recorded. If you let it go, you may find it difficult to complete the entries accurately later. The register acts as a catalogue of all the accessions stored by number.

Computer Systems

A computer system can generate its own register. You will still need some sort of log to make sure that the number you assign is in some sort of succession with all the other numbers and that there are no gaps or duplicates.

The Ledger

The ledger is all the accession information gathered into one place. The old museum ledgers were bound books. If they were complete and accurate, these bound ledgers were excellent devices that kept all the museum registration information in one place. It might be almost impossible to easily extract information from them, but they did store the records better than any other system, even a computer. Some museums use them to this day, in many cases generating them by a computer (see Figure 8). I strongly recommend that you have some type of accession ledger. Your worksheet is a good model for a ledger page (C-4).

An older technology is to write the ledger information in a bound book. This may sound dreadfully old fashioned, but for very small museums this method might be a very viable alternative. Use India or an indelible ink on good paper. An example of a typed ledger page is shown in the appendix (C-6).

It is not a good idea to place all the accession sheets in a file and call that a ledger. Loose files are easily disturbed, records lost, and the whole file misplaced. One reason I recommend a bound book is that it can survive almost any disaster.[2]

You can type your accession sheets in a word processor and create the ledger from that. It strikes me that it is about as easy to type the records into a data base and then you can do many more things with it that you cannot do with a word processor. Most computer programs have a "merge" utility that would allow you to print a register from any word-processing program.

```
Oct 22, 1996                          ACCESSION LEDGER                              Page 1

Acc. Number     Object Name            Description              Comments            Source L Name
---------------  ------------------  -----------------------  -----------------------  -----------------
056.002.001.     Plaque             George Washington; faces viewer's  Artist is an attribution, but  Atterbury Est.
                                    right; profile head and         a good possibility;2/81,
                                    shoulders; in military uniform;  1/8" crack at base of neck
                                    hair in que; set against dark    in front, becoming hairline
                                    chipped crystal ground; oval     halfway across; 1/93,cracked
                                    shadow box with frame of gilded  at neck; frame cracked in
                                    wood; ball molding around edge;  several places; originally
                                    On back is typed label, "This    belonged to Elias Boudinot,
                                    bas-relief of Washington formerly Burlington; list of owners
                                    belonged to Dr. Elias Boudinot   on back;
                                    of Burlington, N.J., and was
                                    bequeathed by him to Lewis
                                    Atterbury, husband of Catherine,
                                    daughter of his [Boudinet's]
                                    brother, Elisha Boudinet. Lewis
                                    Atterbury gave it to his son,
                                    Edward J.C. Atterbury of Trenton,
                                    N.J., and he to his son Albert H.
                                    Atterbury of Plainfield, N.J.
                                    Elias Boudinet's will is recorded
                                    in the Prerogative Court of New
                                    Jersey at Trenton: The
                                    seventeenth paragraph reads: "I
                                    give my nephew, Lewis Atterbury,
                                    the bust of General Washington
                                    taken in white wax."

056.002.006.     Mezzotint          George Washington;head and       4/81 print glued to cardboard;  Atterbury Est.
                                    shoulders; shoulders turned to   removed from frame by Jack
                                    viewer's left and head front;    Koeppel; 7/93, foxed;
                                    "Geo. Washington Esqr. Late
                                    president of the United States of
                                    America'; "From an original
                                    picture in the possession of J.
                                    Seb De Franca Esqr of Devonshire
                                    Place to whom this plate is
                                    dedicated by . . . Robt. Cribb.
                                    [publisher]"; signed "C.G.
                                    Stuart pinxt" lower left and W.
                                    Nutter sculpt" lower right;
                                    "London Published Jany 15 1798 by
                                    Robert Cribb Holborn; framed;
                                    glass painted black with gold
                                    trim to resemble mat;

056.002.00b.     Gun, Market        Probably a Spanish wall gun, as it  Used by Anthony A. Livingston,  Atterbury Est.
                                    has trunions, and later used as a  grandfather of donor; stock
                                    market gun; muzzle loader;       broken in move of 1996.
                                    percussion, but has an unusual

OLD BARRACKS MUSEUM, TRENTON, NEW JERSEY
```

Figure 8. A register printed from a computer data bank. One can print out more information using this medium than with a manual register. The Old Barracks kept a collection ledger for ninety years. Most of the collection is listed in the ledger but not all. The column under the "L" indicates whether it is or is not in the ledger. The column under the "S" is the source; "g" indicates gift, etc. The column under the "C" (for condition) indicates its exhibitability. "a" through "c" are exhibitable. "P" is conservation status. "1" is the lowest status, while "5" indicates that no conservation is needed. "FLG" means "flag." Objects can be flagged to indicate some special status. In this case, "99" indicates the object has been deaccessioned.

Manual Systems

There are several methods of creating a ledger manually. The easiest way is to type up your accession sheets and bind these periodically, say once a year. The advantage of this method is that the technology is simple and cheap.[3]

Computer-Generated Ledger

Generating a ledger from a computer data bank is a relatively easy process using almost any program with which I am familiar (see Figure 9).

Whether it is practical to print all your data out or not is another matter. If you have 10,000 objects the ledger may very well be 10,000 pages long. Bound at 250 pages per book, this is 40 volumes. As the ultimate backup this may be a very useful project, but it may not be too practical. Since computer files are constantly updated this printed ledger can be considered a picture of the collection at one point in time. But what if you have 15,000 objects (60 volumes), or 25,000 objects (100 volumes)? A electronic backup may be a more practical solution. The ledger can be written to the screen very easily. Computers are discussed in Chapter Eight.

Remember this! Data stored in electronic form deteriorate over time, and the programs that read this data do not last indefinitely. The life of a program is typically about five years and companies often do not "support" them for even that length of time. Without the program you may not be able to read the data. Printed on good paper, a written record lasts almost forever. It may pay to print out your whole file once in a lifetime, even if you have a huge collection.

Capturing the Information

Some museums divide the accession information into two separate categories of accession information and catalogue information. Whether the difference has any meaning is moot, but all the information should be written down when the object is accessioned, so I discuss it here. The information is gathered on a worksheet.

Lately museums have been considering a system that will allow one to extract more information from the records than the name of the object. What the content of the record should be was taken up by the Common Agenda Data Bases Task Force in the late 1980s.[4] This was the first real attempt to develop a system with a standard definition of data fields common to all history museums. Not much more work has been done on this concept since then, but it was a worthwhile project and very usable. I show a worksheet made up of the Common Agenda data fields above (see page 60).

```
Feb 5, 1997                          ACCESSION LEDGER                                Page 1

Acc. Number    Object Name          Description                  Comments              Source L Name
------------   ------------------   ------------------------     -----------------     ---------------
056.002.001.   Plaque               George Washington; faces viewer's    Artist is an attribution, but   Atterbury Est.
                                    right; profile head and             a good possibility;2/81,
                                    shoulders; in military uniform;     1/8" crack at base of neck
                                    hair in que; set against dark       in front, becoming hairline
                                    chipped crystal ground; oval        halfway across; 1/93,cracked
                                    shadow box with frame of gilded     at neck; frame cracked in
                                    wood; ball molding around edge;     several places; originally
                                    On back is typed label, "This       belonged to Elias Boudinot,
                                    bas-relief of Washington formerly   Burlington; list of owners
                                    belonged to Dr. Elias Boudinot      on back;
                                    of Burlington, N.J., and was
                                    bequeathed by him to Lewis
                                    Atterbury, husband of Catherine,
                                    daughter of his [Boudinet's]
                                    brother, Elisha Boudinet. Lewis
                                    Atterbury gave it to his son,
                                    Edward J.C. Atterbury of Trenton,
                                    N.J., and he to his son Albert H.
                                    Atterbury of Plainfield, N.J.
                                    Elias Boudinet's will is recorded
                                    in the Prerogative Court of New
                                    Jersey at Trenton: The
                                    seventeenth paragraph reads: "I
                                    give my nephew, Lewis Atterbury,
                                    the bust of General Washington
                                    taken in white wax."

056.002.006.   Mezzotint            George Washington;head and          4/81 print glued to cardboard;  Atterbury Est.
                                    shoulders; shoulders turned to      removed from frame by Jack
                                    viewer's left and head front;       Koeppel; 7/93, foxed;
                                    "Geo. Washington Esqr. Late
                                    president of the United States of
                                    America'; "From an original
                                    picture in the possession of J.
                                    Seb De Franca Esqr of Devonshire
                                    Place to whom this plate is
                                    dedicated by . . . Robt. Cribb.
                                    [publisher]"; signed "C.G.
                                    Stuart pinxt" lower left and W.
                                    Nutter sculpt" lower right;
                                    "London Published Jany 15 1798 by
                                    Robert Cribb Holborn; framed;
                                    glass painted black with gold
                                    trim to resemble mat;

056.002.00b.   Gun, Market          Probably a Spanish wall gun, as it  Used by Anthony A. Livingston,  Atterbury Est.
                                    has trunions, and later used as a   grandfather of donor; stock
                                    market gun; muzzle loader;          broken in move of 1996.
                                    percussion, but has an unusual


OLD BARRACKS MUSEUM, TRENTON, NEW JERSEY
```

Figure 9. An accession ledger printed from a computer data bank. In the interests of saving space, this ledger does not print out all the information on the objects. This contains some of the same objects listed on the register page shown earlier.

As part of the capture of all the information associated with an object, the museum should develop a record form that has a field for each discrete piece of information. A field is one particular piece of information such as the accession number, the name of the object, or the date of manufacture. I suggest some fields in Chapter Eight. The task force has divided the data into major field groups.

Management Data

These are, according to the task force definition, "Data normally recorded or created when an object comes into a collection and data recorded as a means of relating objects and records to one another." This information is what some museums would call "accession" data.

Descriptive Data

The definition of this information is, "Data that can be gathered about an object by observing it or by applying fairly simple research techniques, such as discovering an object's name or title." I like to think that this is information that the object itself tells you. This is what some museums would call "catalogue" data.

Historical Data

Historical data are described as "Data that provide a historical context for objects, relating them to people, organizations, places, events, and concepts." These are the data that are the hardest to acquire but are the most important. I discuss historical data in Chapter Five on documentation.

Descriptions

There is quite a difference between descriptive information written for a manual record and one for a computer. For paper records, compactness and succinctness are plusses. The information is concentrated rather than expanded. A computer may not be able to read a number of abbreviations or handle cryptic notes such as "somewhat like 22.8.6." The computer may well look on such things as a pair of andirons as one object, whereas with a paper record you can easily distinguish that there are two objects.

The information below is mainly for manual records although it useful for both media. For a computer record, some of the information such as size, classification, name, provenance, etc., would go in separate fields. I discuss this in Chapter Eight on computers. I include a worksheet made up of the Common Data Bases

Task Force fields, above, that would be helpful in capturing the information for both media.

The basic part of the record of a properly registered object is the description. Descriptions should be simple and short, but complete enough to be used in court. If you follow the journalistic who, what, where, when, and why, you have a fairly complete description. If you always describe objects using the same criteria in the same order you will not miss much and all your descriptions will be complete. If you set up a data table it makes things easier. A worksheet will do this for you. The computer essentially sets up a data table on screen with all its separate fields.

What: Table, Dining
Classification: Category 2: Furniture
Provenance: New England, perhaps made in Zeus
Association: Jones family; donor says William Jones wrote the town charter on table, ca. 1858
Date: Early 19th century (1810–1830)
Other characteristics: Hepplewhite style
Description: Four tapered legs; rectangular top; outside batten, flush drawer; brass pulls; stained and varnished
Material: Walnut and poplar
Condition: Excellent
Other information: Exhibited in NY Furniture Society exhibit "The New York Cabinetmaker, 1924"; catalogue in acc. file
Size: 64 1/2"w X 38 3/4"d x 29 1/2"h

If written as a description it might look like the sample below. In a computer the information would be in several different fields as shown above.

88.26.1 Table, dining: New England, early 19th century (1810–1830); perhaps local in manufacture; Jones family association; donor says that grandfather (William Jones, 1822–1908) wrote Zeus town charter on this table in ca. 1858; Hepplewhite style; four tapered legs; rectangular top; outside batten; flush drawer with brass pulls; walnut and poplar; stained and varnished; excellent condition; exhibited in the New York Furniture Society exhibit, "The New York Cabinetmaker, 1924"; see catalogue in accession file; see also probate of Adam Jones will in courthouse; 64 1/2"w X 38 3/4"d X 29 1/2"h.

Notice that I qualified several statements in this accession. I used the statement "Donor says. . . ." An oral tradition 140 years old is suspect, but it has been in his family. The donor did not know the exact dates of his grandfather's life, but what information was available is given so that details can be checked later. When I did not know the exact date, I used "ca." for "circa," which means "about."

It is a good idea to do the research on each object as it comes in, before the registration process is completed. The dates his grandfather lived and worked, the courthouse records on its construction, the Collins Axe Company, construction techniques available at the time—all should have been researched. The typical small museum may not have the time to do all this when the accession is made, but the bones of the research will be there, if captured in the first place, and will be available when needed later.

One usually develops a sort of laconic style, leaving out all unnecessary wording. If subjectless or verbless statements separated by semicolons are used, the descriptions are shorter. These descriptions do not have to have any literary merit; they just have to be complete enough to identify that particular object. The descriptions should evoke an accurate picture in the reader's mind, especially if he or she were unfamiliar with the object. Describe what is unique to the object. Short, succinct descriptions are best. The reader of the records has to have some knowledge.

Since using computers, many museums have reduced the description to a few brief comments, or done away with it altogether. This is not a good practice. The first consideration is that the description offers you a way to distinguish new classes of objects. You may be able to extract such information as whether a certain class of table has flush drawers (vs. lipped drawers), which may be significant when compared to other data. The computer offers you a method of making these comparisons quickly, although it can be done with much more difficulty with manual records.

The second consideration is that if the object is stolen you must have a description good enough to distinguish it from all others of its type. You would be surprised how difficult it is to describe to the police how your unique hand-made apple peeler is different from all the other unique hand-made apple peelers.

The final reason for a description is that it helps you identify the object. For one reason or another, you may have to find objects by their descriptions rather than by number or location. The description offers you that method.

If you adopt the policy that the condition of the object will be described as either *pristine, excellent, good, fair*, or *poor* (corresponding to the school marks of A, B, C, D, or E), you save some space. A good practice in manual records is to assume that all objects in the collection are in good ("C") condition unless indicated otherwise, and again you save space. On computer records it would be better to fill in the blank, as the computer will have difficulty differentiating a whether a blank means "C" or nothing.

Measure accurately. On large objects, measure to the sixteenth of an inch, and on small ones measure to the thirty-second. Dudley and Wilkinson recommend measuring to the next largest unit of measurement. That is, if you measure 3 3/16" you then record 3 1/4". That method has a lot to recommend it. Many museums use a metric system and measure to the millimeter. Some museums put both means of measurement in their records but that may be too much for the small museum. Adopt a policy of which system you will use so that one person does not use the inch/foot and the other the metric system. It is easy to configure most data management programs to convert one measurement to the other so that by entering an inch/foot measurement (for instance) you will automatically get the metric measurement.

It is best to take the overall outside measurements in particular order. If you measure the width first, then the depth, and then the height it will help to ensure consistency and simplify your work when you prepare exhibits.

The museum often receives a number of objects that are more or less identical, such as a set of dinner plates. When you are using manual records, it is best to take one object that is typical of all of them and describe it in detail. Then, for the rest, use the abbreviation *ibid.*, which stands for *ibidem* and means "in the same place." *Ibidem* is a Latin word used in scholarly footnotes to refer to the citation before. Its use in the accession records refers only to the description immediately preceding it. If you have a dining room set with twelve matching side chairs, you pick the most typical chair and describe it, then, for the others, you need only to mention minor variations following the word *ibid.* (Actually, *idem*, abbreviated as *id.*, meaning "the same," would be more correct, but I am following the common practice.)

Even if the objects are not enough alike to use the term *ibid.*, it helps to line up similar objects. Then similar or unique characteristics will show up immediately. If you are accessioning a group of costumes, place all the dresses in one pile, all the coats in another, and so on, instead of just grabbing items at random, as they come out of the trunk. (Although if the trunk is still the same order the way it was originally packed, that would be of interest.) You will be amazed at the way this simple method helps descriptions.

If you use a computer for cataloguing, the use of *ibid.* will not work. Computer searches will not know that it is to compare this record with the first in the series, at least in most programs. Even in the unlikely circumstance that the program can make such a search, it would be slower and more prone to errors than if you just give every object its own description. However, the computer gives you the means to copy the first description to all the other records where it is needed.

Describe the usual characteristics and the unusual ones that mark the object. You would be surprised how often descriptions miss the obvious, such as the number of legs on a table. Some objects, such as stamps and coins, are described in catalogues. Referring to the catalogue number can simplify descriptions. Some classes of objects (such as carpenters planes) have a standard scholarly work written about them. Reference to the description in that work can save time. Do not make up words for technical descriptions. If you do not know what a ferrule is, call it a band of metal. Most technical terms come from only four sources—the parts of a human body, nature, mathematics, and architecture. If you learn the terminology for those four sources, you will be explicit even if you do not have the exact term. Clothing and decorative arts have a language all their own that must be learned, eventually if you wish accurate descriptions. Consistency and accuracy are more important than technical vocabulary.

The worksheet, mentioned before, will ensure that you record all the data you need in the order you want it. A worksheet is useful when you are dealing with less knowledgeable people or people in a training status. Even experienced curators will find them useful. There is an example of a worksheet above and in Appendix C-4. You will probably need a worksheet even if the information is stored in a computer. The worksheet does not have to be paper. It can be a screen on the computer.

Almost anything in the world can be described while standing on one foot. The second the other foot touches the ground, stop describing.

Marking Objects

Almost all the work you have done so far on registering an object will be wasted if you do not put the proper accession number on the object. The number ties the object to the records. Marking the object should be part of a definite chain of actions that you perform in the registration process. The process of accessioning should not be considered complete until the number is on the object.[5]

Marking the object is quite a complex process. You will end up with a different technique of marking for each type of object. The marking should not be visible when the object is displayed but should be easily found otherwise. The method of marking should not damage the object. The object should not be marked on finished surfaces. Finally, the number should be firmly attached to the object, so that it will last, but be easily removable if necessary.

Places such as inside the drawer on furniture, the bottom of plates, and the waistband of garments are all logical places to place a number on an object. For tools and implements there may be a problem in finding a hidden place for the number, as the tool may be viewed from any angle. Find as unobtrusive a place as possible. On large pieces, place the number where you will not have to move the piece to find it.

With objects that may occasionally be exposed to the weather, such as an automobile, or become greasy, such as a machine, the number has to be affixed in a very permanent manner. It might be a good idea to screw a brass tag on such objects. It is a good idea to place marks on such pieces in several places. If you are consistent in marking one kind of object in the same place it will help those who follow after. After looking at a few of your accessions they will know where to look the next time the same kind of object comes up.

How you mark each object will vary from object to object. For objects with hard surfaces you may use India ink. Lay down a layer of acrylic and then put on the ink with a pen. You can find Speedball pens with small flat tips that will not scratch. India ink comes in several colors so it can contrast with any surface. That number will survive almost any treatment. It will even go through a dishwasher a couple of times. Yet it can be removed with a few swipes of nail polish remover.

I have used clear nail polish for almost forty years and found it works fine, but conservators are now very much opposed to its use. You can find clear acrylic paints that are acceptable at art supply stores. Conservators strongly recommend Soluvar (Acryloid B-67 + F 10), Acryloid B-72, or polyvinyl Acetate (in denatured alcohol). Sources of supply for these are listed in Appendix D. There are safety concerns in using any finish, or its solvent, in the confines of a museum. Make sure you read all instructions and warnings and have good ventilation. Be certain that anything you use will not damage the surface of the object. It may be necessary to test before using the finish.

Using one of these chemicals you can stick a paper tag with the number or a barcode to the object. This method may become more popular.

On dark surfaces many people place a strip of clear finish, then a strip of white lacquer paint. They write the number on the white with India ink and then apply another stripe of clear lacquer. Many museums prefer this method of marking to any other. Whiteout also comes in handy little bottles with brushes. It will work, but it often reacts with the lacquer you are using, so I do not recommend it. Use a white lacquer. You can get white drawing ink that will save you a step in this situation.

A traditional method is the use of paint. The kinds used by sign painters or model builders are good. Buy the paint in small containers. A red color is good as it is easy to see on most surfaces but not that intrusive. A small (#000 or #0000) brush with a pointed tip works best. Lay down a layer of clear finish as you would with any other method on the object. When the first layer dries, paint the number on the strip of clear lacquer. When that paint dries, put another layer of clear lacquer on top. I like using paint the most, but it is the hardest to use.

Clothing and textiles should not be marked directly on the material. The best method is to sew a strip of cloth on the material and then write the number with a laundry pen. India ink will not work on textiles as it washes out, so use a laundry pen. Paper items should be marked with a soft pencil (#2). These are easily available in stationers stores.

You may not be able to mark coins, medallions, small jewelry items, small pieces of sculpture, etc., that do not have a surface on which it would be proper to place the marking. In the case of coins and medals you can buy special envelopes and mark the number on them. These envelopes are available in any coin shop. You can use small paper tags on jewelry. Small sculpture may have to be kept resting on a tag with its number. When the number is not placed on the object special care must be taken not to separate the tag from the object.

Glued-on paper labels, especially ones that are pressure sensitive, are a very poor choice. So are those neat long strips of plastic that you can number from a machine. The adhesives break down rapidly and may damage the object. The labels have a perverse way of dropping off at the most inconvenient moment, and then not being removable at other times. Clear cellophane or similar tapes should never be used.

Paper tags held on with string are very useful as a second marker but not as the permanent one. Objects in storage will be easier to find with paper tags, and that may be a reason to use them. They should never be considered the sole means of marking objects as they are removed too easily. However, paper labels can be used. The number is written on the label and then a layer of lacquer is applied. The label is applied wet. When the lacquer dries a second layer of lacquer is applied. This will work with barcodes.

Deaccessioning

The question in deaccessioning is not if there is going to be a problem, but when there will be one.

With deaccessioning, it is the *accessioning* policy that is important. If you are careful what you bring in, you will have fewer objects to dispose. The development

development of a sound accession policy, the careful execution of procedures, and good records will put off the evil day and lessen any problem with deaccessioning when it occurs. However, there is hardly a museum in the country that does not depend on the good will of its audience for survival. That good will is often expressed in gifts to the museum. When offered objects, the museum is under an obligation to accept only what it really needs, can really take care of, has a use for, and intends to keep.[1]

There is a Justification for Accessions form in Appendix C-13 that represents a procedure for evaluating objects *before* accessioning and will help the museum decide to accept or reject items offered to it. Using this procedure will help you acquire objects less likely to be deaccessioned later.

No matter how carefully written the collection policy of a museum may be, or how tightly that policy is enforced, there is no museum that does not occasionally end up with objects that do not belong in the collection:

- There may be too many of one kind of object.
- The object may not fit the collection policy.
- It may have deteriorated to the point where it has lost its integrity or is a threat to the collection.
- It may be a fake (or at least not as represented).
- The museum may not be able to take care of the object properly.

For these reasons, museums remove objects from their collections, or deaccession them.

It is a poor policy for the museum to dispose of objects in its collection unless there is an overriding reason for doing so. I would recommend not deaccessioning an object from a living donor, or one that has a known history related to your purpose, unless it is deteriorated to the point that it endangers the collection.

It is important to follow a set procedure in deaccessioning and to be able to justify all the steps. There is a Justification for Deaccessioning form in the appendix (C-14). Thus, each of the two collections policies in the appendix have a deaccession procedure including a Justification for Deaccessioning form. There should be a clearly understood policy about how the object is to be disposed of. Using the form, or the procedure it represents, will help the museum have a rational method of deaccessioning and keep the collection germane to the purpose of the museum.

When you take something in your collection, you should at the same time think about how it might be removed without creating confusion in the records. The governing body should make the deaccession policy a part of the registration manual. Any action to get rid of an object should be done only after the governing body acts. The easiest way to get such action is to have the curator, through the director, recommend to the collections committee that the object be deaccessioned, who then make a report to the board concerning the object, the reasons for the deaccession, and the method of disposal. If the board approves, the action is carried out.

You should not get rid of the records for the object that has been deaccessioned just because the object is gone. You are still obligated to keep the record of it. For paper records a note indicating that the object has been deaccessioned should be made in red ink in the master record. The reason for using red ink for this transaction on the records is that it will show up clearly. India ink should be used. The type of removal (sold, destroyed, transferred), the date it happened, and the date of the action of the governing body should all be entered into the permanent record. If you have catalogue cards for the deaccessioned object they should be placed in a dead file. There should be some method in a computer record to indicate that the object has been deaccessioned and a method of keeping it from getting mixed with the rest of the records, but, again, the record should be kept.

Under both the AAM and AASLH ethics codes, funds received from the sale of accessioned items can go only to buy other artifacts or toward the conservation of objects in the collection. This should be addressed in your collection policy.

Although the museum board should reserve the right to dispose of the collection in any way it sees fit, in actual practice the museum will be rated on how much it keeps and keeps well.

I could write a whole book on donor and community concerns involved in deaccessioning. The museum has to carefully consider what impact any deaccession will have on its relationship, with its donors, and the community. Every deaccession represents some failure on the part of the museum. However, deaccessioning is very much like pruning a tree; it hurts, but is necessary for growth. If the museum carefully considers each deaccession, the problems will be fewer.

Tiered Collections

Museums often have objects that they wish to keep but not accession. Typically, these are used in education programs or are kept for study. In these cases museums often create a tiered system. There may be anywhere from two to a dozen tiers. The museum designates one or two tiers in which the object is accessioned and cared for under the highest museum standards. Other tiers may not be technically accessioned, but may be used in education programs or kept as specimens. These often get a special numbering system and may be kept in different ledgers.

This arrangement will work, but the museum has to have a very good understanding of its mission and the role of the collection. The ability to administer such a system is important. Someone has to constantly monitor the use of objects so that everyone will understand that you can use objects marked with an "X" (for example) and may not use ones that are not.

Be aware that if you take in an object from a donor under the impression that it is to be a "museum" object and then place it in noncollection status, you have created a sizable ethical and perhaps legal problem. Be up front about the status of any object you take into your collection, whether accessioned or not.

What Not to Do and When Not to Do It

The major mistake people make is to not accession the object as soon as it comes in. If it is not accessioned promptly information will be lost, parts may turn up missing, or the object may not be accessioned at all. I have always been amazed, at the museums where I had collection responsibilities, how many objects sat around for years without being accessioned. The final mistake is to not put the number on the object at the same time it is accessioned.

The Final Word on Accessioning

Several variations of the basic system of accessioning have been outlined here to help the person in charge understand them and assist him or her in setting up their own system. The important things about any system are that:

- The flow of actions is orderly and uncomplicated from the first contact until the object is displayed or stored.
- The museum is able to account for any action at any stage of the process.
- The system is consistent.
- The system is understood and approved of by the people directing and managing the museum.
- The system can be carried out over a number of years through the reigns of several curators.

The records of the museum are only tools meant to help you preserve and interpret the collection. Do not create a monster that will eat up the purpose of the museum in a maze of paperwork. Simplicity is the key.

NOTES

1. Malaro, *Legal Primer*, pp. 52–137. The whole registration process is in Dudley and Wilkinson, pp. 21–39. Margot M. Pearsall and Holly B. Ulseth, *Registration Records in a History Museum, ibid.,* pp. 245–252, discuss the system in which I was trained. See also Antony J. Duggan, "Collection Management," in John M. A. Thompson, *Manual for Curatorship: A Guide for Museum Practice* (London: Butterworth, 1984), pp. 113–376.

2. You can also get a type of record called a "minute book," that has loose pages. The pages can be permanently fixed later, but can be edited or copied until bound.

3. For the reasons to not put the accession record on a card, see Chapter Six, p. 102, on catalogues.

4. James C. Blackaby, Chair, Common Data Bases Task Force, *Final Report to the Field, September, 1989,* Common Agenda for History Museums (Nashville: AASLH, 1989). This is a corrected version of James R. Blackaby, Chair, "Managing Historical Data: Report of the Common Agenda Task Force," *Special Report 3* (Nashville: AASLH, 1989).

5. Dudley and Wilkinson, pp. 41–62 and *passim,* on measuring and marking objects is excellent. The information on modern marking materials comes from the Conservation Center, Pennsylvania Historical and Museum Commission.

6. Phelan, *Guide,* pp. 302–306; Charles Philips, "The Ins and Outs of Deaccessioning," *History News,* 58, 5 (May/June 1983), pp. 24–20; Stephen Weil, "Deaccession Practices in American Museums," *Museum News,* 65, 3 (February 1987), pp. 44–50; Malaro, *Primer,* pp. 138–155 and *passim.* Dudley and Wilkinson discuss deaccession files, pp. 35–36. The New York Association of Museums, "Guidelines on Deaccessioning," are shown in Phelan, *Museum Law,* pp. 241–242. There is an excellent letter to the editor by Steven Miller, "Deaccessioning as Destruction," *Museum News,* 69, 5 (September/ October 1990), pp. 7–8. I am in total agreement with the thoughts expressed in this letter, the tenor of which may be seen in the title. See also Miller, "Selling Items from Museum Collections," *International Journal of Museum Management and Curatorship* 4 (1985), pp. 289–294.

Five

Documentation

When you acquire an object you acquire a great deal more than the object itself. You acquire the history of the people who made or used the object. This legacy is often more valuable to the museum than the intrinsic value of the object. The very difference between a history museum and other types of museums is often that they collect objects for their historical value rather than for their intrinsic, aesthetic, or scientific values. Of course, these other values are important and are major factors in all museum collections, but they are not the primary value. The only way to preserve this value is to write it down. This written history is the documentation of the object and the collection.

In the United States, it is normal to separate registration from documentation. The usual practice is to consider that registration applies to all the records generated in the acquisition, accession, and catalogue process and that documentation applies to research developed on the object and the collection. Be aware that some people in the museum field apply the term "documentation" to all the documents developed on an accession or the collection. They expressly include the ones I separate as "registration" documents. This usage is more true of Great Britain than the United States, although "documentation" as applied to registration is often used here. I separate the two terms in this book, partly to follow the common practice in the United States, and partly to avoid confusion. For the purposes of this book, "documentation" is part of the registration process, not the process itself.[1]

You acquire information on the object in two ways. Some information comes with the object. The rest is found by research.

Information that Comes with the Object

The donor or seller of an object will often furnish you with information about the object. There will frequently be the owner's reminiscences or family history. If you question donors they can often give you an amazing amount of background information. It is important to capture all of this history that you can. Ask for photographs, documents, and other things related to the object. The owner will not know they are important.

You should be aware of all the pitfalls of oral information. Nothing ever became less important or less valuable over time. Still, if it is the original owner, or a descendent who provides the information, it is close to the source. Almost all oral information is lost when the object is sold to a dealer or second party. Any history coming from such second-party sources is suspect, especially if it is an unsupported attribution to an owner, artist, or maker.

However unlikely some of this information may be, if you do not collect it at the time of the accession it will be forever lost. All of it should be carefully recorded. You can check out the information later through research.

Information Discovered by Research

The museum should have an ongoing research project concerning the history covered by the museum's purpose. If your purpose is to preserve the history of Hero County, you would continually conduct research on the history of the county. Research is never completed.

You also must conduct research on the objects in the museum. Who made or used them, when they made them, and how they were used will be constant topics of research. You must also learn something about the cultural and aesthetic motives of the people who made and used the objects and the technical qualities of the object. Research will give you a greater understanding of the people associated with your collection and be of enormous help in collection, interpretation, and exhibition.

Registration Files vs. Research Files

Even the smallest museum may have several types of documents that ought to be preserved. It is common to have the accession file that contains all the documents on each object, a research file that contains research on the history related to the museum's purpose, the archives, which contain documents in the museum's collection, and the museum files that are business and other records.[2] It is good to keep separate files, but all of these should be preserved as museum archives.

The major difference between archives and business files is the type of care they receive and how you intend to preserve them. The archives, of whatever kind, are part of the museum's collection. Although archives are used for research, they receive the highest standard of care the museum can devise. It may be stored separately, but the museum registration system is part of the museum's archives. Sometimes research files are files that do not receive the same care that the archives do. In this case, you should make sure that documents that are to be preserved go into the archives or at least get a high standard of care.

Documents that come with objects are part of the museum archives. If these are stored in accession files, be sure that these files follow archive standards. If the documents are used frequently, then they should be copied, the copies placed in the research files, and the originals preserved.

Some documents are as much a part of the accession as the object itself. These might be operating manuals, original letters referring to the object, photographs that show the object in use, legal documents concerning it, etc. You must make a decision on which of these are accessioned, which go into the accession file, which into the research file, and which to the museum archives. The decision is based on the standard of care you give each file and, perhaps, who has access to it.

The Museum Library

The museum should develop a library on its collection. A small book budget will go a long way. If you collect a book here and there, eventually you will have a good reference library. Books are expensive, but many are remaindered and can be acquired cheaply. Donors are often quite generous with books. When I started at Old Economy I had 8 books in the museum reference library. When I left sixteen years later, there were over 2,000 books in the library and I never, in that whole time, had a book budget. If I had had a book budget, I would have had 4,000 books. Keep at it and eventually your efforts will show results.

Publishing Research

Research is not good unless it is published. The museum publishes in many ways. Exhibits and interpretation programs can be considered methods of publication that are especially suited to a museum. Every exhibit requires some research, and if this is published it will add another dimension to the exhibit. Even a simple fact sheet will outlast the exhibit and be a permanent remainder of your research. Even if it has to be done on the office copier, it is still a publication. The museum should publish articles and monographs on its collection. Your newsletter is a good place to publish what you have found. Another way to publish is to encourage and assist outside researchers. Their publications should be added to your library. Remember that exhibits and interpretation programs, although valuable and necessary, are ephemeral, but publications last forever.

Interest Groups

There is an interest group on almost any subject, no matter how obscure; I once subscribed to a magazine for plumb bob collectors. These groups have publications, meetings, memberships, etc. There must be at least one, if not a dozen, of these groups whose interests are aligned with those of any museum. These groups will be conversant with current research and standards in their field. They will know all the specialists in the obscure areas of their interest. They will know all the good books on their specialty and how to get discounts. I suggest that the museum join as many of these interest groups as you need and can afford. Go to as many of their meetings as you can. Their annual meetings are information factories where you can find out almost anything you need to know. You will discover the state of current knowledge when you do this.

Information from Other Museums

Other museums that collect in the same area as yours can be quite helpful. They will have a research file and a library. Their professional staff will be conversant with the knowledge you need. Museums lend objects as well, and may be able to help you with exhibits.

On the other hand, it is a common experience in a large museum for someone from the Out-of-the-Way Historical Society to show up unannounced at the most inconvenient moment and seek highly specialized knowledge. The seeker might be put off by curt answers and hasty references to standard reference works, but you can hardly expect a curator to impart all the knowledge they have gained in a lifetime in twenty minutes. Contact the museum in advance, tell them what you would like to know, and you will usually find them very helpful.

A number of computer networks that are being developed now may offer museums access to information about objects and collections. This is particularly true for art museums at this time. If this trend follows the course of similar affinity groups and associations, then it may prove quite useful. It is too early to say just what will happen in this area for history museums, but it is bright with promise.

Higher Standards

The museum profession is now placing a much higher value on capturing the historical data on the object than it has in the past. The very nature of a history museum, of being more interested in the object's history than in the object as a specimen, makes this an imperative. One of the main concerns that the Common Data Bases Task Force for the Common Agenda addressed was just such an issue.

What Not to Do and When Not to Do It

The first mistake is not to get all the information at the time you acquire the object. The second mistake is not to write it down. I once ran a museum with almost 80,000 objects related to a particular culture. Each object had a story, but that story was lost as it was in the heads of the founders, who had died thirty years before. It is a general rule, that if you do not capture the information at first, it is lost forever. Since the history museum may be more interested in the history of the object than the object itself, you have an obligation to find all you can about the object and write this down in some easily accessible form. If you have done this on every object, you may have preserved something as valuable as the object itself.

NOTES

1. There is a difference of opinion over what the term "documentation" means. The common view in the United States is that documentation is the assemblage of all the research information on the object. The American use of the term can be seen in Dudley and Wilkinson, where there is no listing in the index for documentation, and under "documents" one is referred to "manuscripts." Europeans view it as all the documents assembled during the whole registration process. I tend to accept the former view. Compare Museum Documentation Association, *Practical Museum Documentation*, 2nd ed. (Duxford, Cambridgeshire: MDA, 1981) with Frederick L. Rath and Merrilyn R. O'Connell, eds., *A Bibliography on Historical Organization Practices*, Vol. 4, *Documentation of Collections* (Nashville: AASLH, 1979). However, one of the first practical books aimed at American museums, Carl E. Guthe, *The Management of Small History Museums*, 2nd ed. (Nashville: AASLH, 1969), pp. 21–50, discusses the entire registration system as documentation.

2. William A. Deiss, *Museum Archives: An Introduction* (Chicago: Society of American Archivists, 1984), discusses museum archives as separate from other archives; James Sumerville, "Using, Managing and Preserving the Records of Your Historical Organization," *Technical Report 11* (Nashville: AASLH, 1986).

Six

The Catalogue

The catalogue[1] is the mechanism that allows you to extract useful information from the museum records.[2] The catalogue divides the information in your records into useful classes or categories and provides the tool for access to this data. At one time, this mechanism would have been a card catalogue. With the advent of the computer, the concept of what a museum catalogue is has been expanded and access to both the records and the collection has been greatly extended. Despite this, the card catalogue survives in many museums—some are even generated by a computer. Regardless of the radically different media used in storing catalogues, there is not a lot of difference among them in the type of data stored. I am going to discuss both manual and electronic catalogues.

The term "catalogue" comes from the ancient Greek and means to count down, with the idea of counting completely. The first catalogues, as we know them, were developed in the Hellenistic period in the famous library at Alexandria. One of the interesting concepts was developed by a man named Calimachus who arranged the catalogue by author in alphabetical order—a revolutionary idea at the time. Librarians have been thinking about catalogues ever since. The first museum ledgers that we know about were developed in the Renaissance. These listed the objects in some arbitrary order, usually the order received. Early attempts at cataloguing included keeping separate ledgers for different types of objects or for different collections.[3]

Until relatively recently, a ledger was the preferred method of storing collection records. An accession ledger (whether written or electronic), accession sheets, and similar forms store almost all the information the museum has on its collection in their mass. They are useful records, and one would hardly be considered a museum without them, but it is very difficult to easily extract data from them. The catalogue is the easy and safe access to all this information.

It would be interesting to know who first took the information in the accession ledger, wrote out each record on a separate piece of paper or card, and arranged these into categories to give useful information. If we knew who that person was, we should erect a statue of him or her, because that solved the problem of how to access the huge mass of information in the museum's records. The cards can be placed in endless combinations allowing for almost limitless searches for the information in the museum records. It was as revolutionary an idea as Calimachus arranging the catalogue alphabetically by author in the third century BC.

The cards were also a curse. They multiplied like flies; they were difficult to create; they occupied a lot of space; they stored endless amounts of redundant data; they were in multiple forms; people mixed them up, lost them, and misplaced them; and they sometimes contained inaccurate data deep in their depths.

Now, of course, we have computers. The computer's ability to sort and index data, its ability to pull together related pieces of information, the lack of redundancy, and especially the speed, make it the ultimate cataloguing tool. A great advantage of the computer is that you need few, if any, forms. Instead of having information stored on a number of pieces of paper and these in a number of places, the computer can store the information in one place to which access is a lot faster and easier. Inaccurate information is even more of a problem in a computer than in a card file, but the computer can often identify some of its own errors.

I do not use a card catalogue any more. I can extract more useful information from my data bank, either on the screen or by a written report, than could easily be extracted from any card catalogue.

Even with a computer, however, a card catalogue may have uses. A card might be considered an analog while a computer is digital. When there is a problem, you can spread all the doubtful cards on the desk and see the whole problem. With a computer, you see one record. When the computer is down, the card catalogue is a good backup. When you need just one or two objects from storage, it's much easier to take a card or two with you rather than a thick printout. If the collection is static and does not change much, a card catalogue might be useful. If there is limited access to the computer, a card catalogue might be a supplement to the computer, allowing more people admission to the records. If the collection is small, a card catalogue might be a lot easier to use than a computer. A card catalogue can provide a safe public access to the records. Finally, some people are more comfortable with paper records than with electronic ones.

On the other hand, if the collection is large or is constantly growing, if the records are being updated, if the records are audited frequently, or if one needs to make sophisticated searches, a computer data bank will be a lot more useful than a paper catalogue. If you have a large collection, you may wish to consider whether you want to have a paper catalogue at all.

I expect to see the catalogue card almost completely replaced by the computer in my lifetime, if that has not happened already.

What Does the Catalogue Tell You?

What does a catalogue tell you? That depends on what you need to know. Some questions can be fairly obscure, such as, "What objects are there, and where are they, which tell me something about the Industrial Revolution in Hero County?" Some questions are fairly simple, such as, "Where are all the Windsor chairs?" Others are more complicated such as, "Is there a relationship between tapered legs and lipped drawers on tables made in Hero County before 1810?" Even a paper catalogue can give you this information, though it may be harder to dig out than it would from a computer. If you are going to have a simple finding aid, then you do not need much information in the catalogue. If you want a complete registration file, then you need more.

Cataloguing Involves Two Different Concepts

For all that people spend a great deal of time cataloguing a museum collection, the definition of the act of cataloguing is rather vague and there is no agreement on the definition. There are actually several different processes that are called cataloguing. They mainly fall into two classes:

1. The creation of the catalogue by extracting data from your records and presenting it in some useful format.
2. The updating of the information in the collection records. Every generation of professionals that works with the collection expands the museum's knowledge about the collection. If this new understanding of the collection is written into the permanent records it will destroy primary data. Therefore, the new information is written into the catalogue. Often a completely new catalogue is created and then becomes the record of choice. When people talk about cataloguing, they are usually talking about this updating process.

When you enter new data into a catalogue you may be destroying some of the old information. This old information may be valuable. To get around this problem the museum should archive the old paper records or periodically archive a copy of its computer records. For most museums, archiving the computer records once a year is enough. For large active collections that are constantly being updated more often may be necessary, say every month.

Classification

No catalogue system will work well unless there is at least one constant used to classify the objects. The reason for this is that the constant gives you the ability to classify the whole file in some rational order. Using a constant you can deal with the collection as a whole. Different disciplines use different classification criteria:

- Art museums use artist, but also period, medium, or genre.
- Natural history museums use a taxonomy based a system first developed by Linnaeus (Karl Linné, 1707–1778).
- Earth science museums use geological epochs or chemical composition.

Until recently, history museums did not have a classification system. The favored classifications for many years was the material of which the object was made (such as "silver"), broad topical classes ("tools"), style ("Hepplewhite"), or, in large museums, by the department that was responsible for the collection ("Social History").

It was not until Robert Chenhall[4] created his system in the 1970s that the idea of a systematic catalogue in a history museum came about. The system would be a standard taxonomy common across the whole history field and useful to anyone. To a great extent, Chenhall's dream of a systematic classification system has been adopted by the history museum field. I will refer to Chenhall's *Revised Edition* as *Nomenclature*. This system of classification arranges objects by their use and has simple naming conventions. By using *Nomenclature* you can arrange your collection in a meaningful order that is understandable by any rational person.

The reason to use a widely accepted classification system is that it is readily understandable by many people in the museum field. A new curator or a visiting scholar will be able to understand your system with little instruction. Besides, *Nomenclature* is fairly simple. If the museum develops its own classification system, it is a lot harder to learn and may not be consistent over many changes of staff.

There are new systems that challenge the concept that you need a constant for a registration system. The cry is to let the computer make its own classification. With the right kinds of data, many systems can do just that.[5] Please note that a numbering system is not a classification system, even though you can arrange your system by number. It's just a method of registering each object.

How *Nomenclature* Works

Nomenclature classifies a collection based on how the objects are used. It has the terms arranged in a taxonomy.[6]

If you know a bit about furniture, you might describe a typical large case piece as either a Kass, a Schrank, a Wardrobe, a Press, an Armoire, or whatever. Even if the catalogue entries bearing these terms were all filed under "Wardrobe," this will cause confusion. A person from the part of the country I come from will call a certain iron cooking utensil a "skillet," whereas someone from another part might call it a "frying pan." Both terms are correct. Do you drive a car or an automobile? The number of synonyms does not matter in speaking or writing, it but does when you are classifying your collection. *Nomenclature* uses only one term for each object. Furthermore, these terms are arranged in broad families based on their use. This allows you to find records quickly. Unlike many of the old classification systems, certain types of objects could appear in every one of *Nomenclature's* families. Most trades or skills use a hammer. These hammers are each filed separately under their use, while in the old days they would all be filed together under "hammers."

Nomenclature systematizes the naming of terms we use in identifying objects that are made by people. The system is not particularly difficult to adopt, even for a small museum. You have to recognize that Chenhall did not create just a list of approved terms, but a whole system of classification of objects for history museums.

As an example, you may have five common bench planes: a smoothing plane, a jack plane, a fore plane, a jointer, and a long jointer. Filed alphabetically, these names would be scattered in several places in the catalogue:

fore plane (in the F's)
jack plane (in the J's)
jointer plane (in the J's)
long jointer (in the L's)
smoothing plane (in the S's)

This would make searches difficult, at best, as you would have to know exactly what you were looking for in order to find it. However, if you followed the principles in *Nomenclature* and treated the noun as a genus (class) and the modifier as a species (type), you would have them arranged thusly:

plane, fore
plane, jack
plane, jointer
plane, long jointer
plane, smoothing

These tools would be filed under a family name of "Tools and Equipment for Materials, Woodworking"; you would always be able to find them in one particular place, so long as you knew their use.

It is true that the nature of the English language causes problems. Objects such as a teaspoon ("spoon, tea"?) or a football ("ball, foot"?) will not neatly arrange themselves, but in the worst cases you can use a cross-reference.

The lexicon is a list of words arranged in some logical order. *Nomenclature* is pretty lengthy, and many of the terms may not be relevant to your collection, so it is easier to develop your own using its principles.

If you have a computer, you can generate a word list that will be the basis of a nomenclature. Some systems will do word counts for you that will simplify the process. It is a little more difficult with a manual system. A relatively easy way for your museum to set up a nomenclature with a manual system is to go through your catalogue. Each term should be compared against *Nomenclature*'s list. If it is not on the list then you have to create a term. *Nomenclature* explains how to do this.

Enter the term on a card. It helps if you put the accession number for the first use on the card. This will help with later descriptions. The first use is technically the first time you used the term. If you are working with an existing catalogue it will probably be the first time you run across the term. You need to enter each term only once. In a collection of 15,000 items I used only about 500 terms, whereas *Nomenclature* lists over 5,000.

Some museums have a separate listing of their catalogue headings. These listings often become part of the registrar's manual or of the operating procedures of the museum. That helps avoid duplication, is especially handy with large staff, and may be necessary if the museum is developing a nomenclature. However, I really do not think a small museum has to worry about listing its headings separately. That is just one more thing to take care of, and if you really want to know what your headings are, you can look in the catalogue drawer or in your computer's data bank. *Nomenclature* supplies a set of ready-made headings for you.

If you color-code your dividing cards so that you can tell the main heading from the subheadings it is easier. Cards are filed by accession number inside each classification.

What Catalogues Do You Need?

If you follow the concepts in this book, the basic records of your museum registration system that we have developed so far will consist of:

Transfer-of-title document consisting of a gift agreement, bill of sale, or some other document transferring title to the museum.

Accessions Register containing the accession number, brief description of what is in the accession, the source, the method of acquisition, and the date of acquisition. The ledger may serve as this document.

Accession Record on each object in the accession. This would include all the information you have on the object. These records should be bound into an accession ledger or book.

Accession File consisting of correspondence, research notes, documents, and other records of each accession in a file.

You will need these records if you are writing them into a bound ledger with a quill pen, or typing them into a paperless system on a computer, or every technique in-between. I am certain I could get a small museum accredited by the AASLH with no more collection records than these primary records, provided the records were complete and accurate. However, as I have emphasized several times, you do not wish to continually use your primary records. The catalogue not only protects these records but gives you access to them.

I am going to discuss manual (or paper) catalogues separately from ones generated by computer.

Manual Catalogues

It is impossible to advise anyone on which catalogues to have without talking to them and seeing the museum and its needs. I suggest the following catalogues are the minimum that any museum needs.

Main Entry Catalogue

A main entry is the card or record upon which any other type of record in the catalogue is modeled. In fact, the easiest way to make other catalogues is to copy the main entry card (see Figure 10).

Object: Plate, Dinner   **Acc. No.**: 52.2.1
Class.: 04 Food Service
Source: Ivy Propan
Location: 101
Material: Pottery   **Size**: 11.375 dia. x .875
Maker: Clews   **Place**: England
Date: ca. 1830   **Association**: Lafayette

Description:
Flat Bowl with curving sides; marly curves up; lip faintly scalloped; foot ring; underglaze blue transfer of landing of Lafayette over white ground; on bottom is stamp between two circles, "Clews Warranted safe [illegible]"; and, in underglaze blue, "The Landing of Lafayette at Castle Garden New York 16th August 1824."

HERO COUNTY HISTORICAL MUSEUM[7]

Figure 10. Main entry card.

The main entry card contains most of the catalogue information. Just what catalogue information is is mostly up to you, but it would logically consist of the accession number, the source, and the descriptive information. This type of information is discussed in Chapter Four. If you have only one catalogue, use a main entry card, and all of your cards are arranged by *Nomenclature*'s principles, then you can answer such complicated questions as, "What furniture do we have that was made in Hero County before 1800 by known cabinet makers?" When you can answer that kind of sophisticated question from the main entry catalogue, you have to question the wisdom of having several.

If there are photographs of the collection, the place to put one of them is on the main entry card. It saves looking in another catalogue for an image.

The Source or Donor Catalogue

The second of the catalogues necessary to operate the museum is the donor or source catalogue. Keep in mind that the sources of funds for purchases are also donors. You may wish to keep a list of vendors as well. Museums that depend on donors for most of their accessions will find themselves constantly using such a file. It is easy to make up, since all you need is a brief description of the accession and the accession number. All the other information is in the accession records. Figure 11 shows how a donor card might look.

```
Truck, Mr. & Mrs. Mack (Dorothy)

56.36 Toolbox and tools
62.33 Garments, family papers, photos
75.8   Dining room table and chairs
82.27 Misc. household items 1925–1940
93.21 Mrs. Truck's wedding dress
```

Figure 11. Sample donor card.

The example shown is from a three-number system. On the single-number and two-number systems, you would have to enter a range of numbers that cover the accession, for example; see Figures 12 and 13.

The donor cards can easily be made up periodically, such as the end of the month. There should only be one card for each source.

Lexicon

The catalogue will work only if the access to it is easy and the information is accurate. The catalogue should not be a file that only one or two people can use, but be understandable to anyone. I have already discussed the need for a

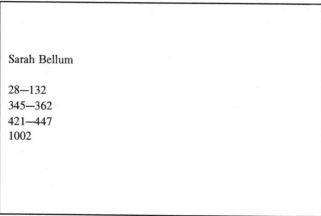

Figure 12. Single-number system.

Figure 13. Two-number system.

nomenclature. Nomenclature and lexicon are interchangeable terms, but many people in the museum field use the term lexicon for the device that holds nomenclature. The discipline of the nomenclature can force the museum to adopt a rational category system that is easy to use. That is why it is advocated so heavily by professionals in the field.

The lexicon can be stored on cards. In the absence of any technology more advanced than a typewriter, this may be the only method. The idea of a standard nomenclature came from the first attempts to computerize history collections. A system stored in a computer should be able to generate a lexicon of itself and be able to be easily corrected and updated. The general utility of a nomenclature becomes obvious to all of those who use it. Whether your system will ever be in some electronic data form or not, I believe that the nomenclature is a necessity.

Even in a large collection, the curator will quickly become familiar with all the terms used in the nomenclature. A quick reference to the list will be needed to check on unfamiliar terms. Such a nomenclature actually takes little time to implement if you develop one from the beginning of the museum's registration system. If you already have a large catalogue, developing a lexicon may be a real problem requiring a complicated system of cross references. New terms will have to be added as you add to your collection in order to keep the list up-to-date and accurate.

Location Catalogue

Because good museum practice requires that you place your hands on any object at short notice, one of the things you need to know is the location of each object in your museum. The standard method is to write the location in pencil on your main entry card. Every time you move the object you change the location. This can be a complicated and time-consuming task.

Another method is to have a card on each object filed by location. When you move the object you move the card. This is handy when someone asks you about the spittoon in the main room, or when doing inventories; you can find the card you need quite easily. The problem with a separate card file for location is that you can't find the location from the Main Entry Catalogue, so you still have to have the location in pencil on that card as well, which means you are keeping the location in two places. If you can support that, a separate location catalogue is quite handy. One of the advantages of a computerized registration system is its ability to easily generate a location catalogue.

Partly to resolve these problems, and partly because you can't write a location on a computer record in pencil, a system of having objects "live" at one location was developed. The object is assigned a permanent location where it "lives." The only time the location is tracked is when the object is moved. This system has a lot to recommend it.

Whether you have a separate location catalogue or not, it is useful to have a catalogue of each exhibit room. These are handy references when visitors ask questions. There are several ways to do this. One is to keep a card file in the room containing a copy of the main entry card. If the object is moved, so is the card.

Most museums using this system favor small ring-bound books as they are easy to hide, yet handy. You can copy all your cards onto the pages, or type the information needed.

Association Catalogue

Part of the information that gives an object value is its association with people, places, or events. The association is often more important than the object itself. A silk hat is a silk hat, but if had been Abraham Lincoln's silk hat. . . ! An object may have a manufacturer's name on it, may be associated with a particular event, such as the Civil War, or with a particular place, such as the local reform school. An easy way to access the knowledge of this association can be a valuable aid in research and developing exhibits. An association catalogue can help you do this.

Association cards are somewhat like donor cards, but they have to have the title of the object as well as the name of the association and the accession numbers. A typical example would look like Figure 14.

Gomorra Pool Hall
Main Street, Hero (1929–1979)

62.29.27 Pool cue
70.2.3   Snooker championship cup
77.38.1   photo of "gang" at hall
76.99.8   Scrapbook of trial

Cross Ref. Lott, G. D. (owner), Main Street, Recreation, Billiard halls

HERO COUNTY HISTORICAL SOCIETY

Figure 14. Example of association card.

When you plan to make an exhibit on Main Street, or on recreation in Hero, or on pool halls, or on G. D. Lott, you can look up the information in your association file. This file is easier to make up if you note the association on your Accession Record. Even if you cannot make up an association file now, the information will be readily available when you can.

Exhibit Catalogues

It may be a good idea to have a catalogue of the objects on exhibit. This is handy when a question comes up, when tracking conditions, and later, after the exhibit comes down, the catalogue is a permanent record of what was in the exhibit. It can be in any form, but it may be best typed up on sheets and filed with the other material on the exhibit. The simplest is to xerox the cards on to a sheet of paper. I generate a complete catalogue of the items in each exhibit from my data bank. If a question comes up, I can then find all the information I need in one place. In the old days I xeroxed the catalogue cards.

Photographs of the Collection

The trite saying about a picture being worth a thousand words is particularly true of a registration system. A photograph makes any description much clearer and can help greatly in identifying objects. Photographs are also useful in showing condition.

The photographic image should be associated with the object. The accession number should be photographed along with the object and be part of the image. Two contact prints should be made of each roll of film. Cut up one of these into individual shots. Attach each shot to the back of the proper catalogue card. Use a glue that will not deteriorate or creep. Dry mounting is best, but a high quality carpenter's glue will do. Many archival supply houses sell neutral pH pastes or glues that will work adequately for this purpose. Never use mucilage or rubber cement. The second contact print is filed with the negatives.

Equipment to take good photographs of the collection is readily available, inexpensive, and easy to operate. If the museum staff does not have the expertise or time, there are many people who do. They may photograph objects for you for the price of the film. It is best to photograph each object in the collection as it is accessioned. If that is impossible, try to photograph the more important objects.

The purpose of the photograph is for identification. Although a good photograph is desirable, you are not turning out a work of art. Each object should be photographed individually, as it is almost impossible to photograph a group of objects well enough for identification purposes. A contact print should be made of the negative from each and the negative fastened in a sleeve on the back. These sleeves are readily available from archive supply houses.

Some museums have a separate catalogue for photographs of the collection. This is a lot of work, but may be necessary for certain collections. One way to have such a catalogue is to have a print made of each object the same size as the file drawer, say 3 by 5″, and file them in accession number order. The information you need can be printed on the back.

If you have a rubber stamp made containing the information you need, the job becomes much easier. With a computer you can generate a label that will do the same thing. The negative is more important than the prints, so keeping track of them is important. See Figure 15, which shows how a typical stamp might look.

HERO COUNTY MUSEUM
Photographic File

Acc. No. ___68.26.1_____
Neg. No. ___0300877.1.1__ [8]
Object _____Horseshoe____

Figure 15. Example of rubber stamp.

Photo Imaging

There are a number of ways to store images electronically. These systems are very valuable as you can bring up the image with the catalogue record. The technology is evolving rapidly and is getting cheaper and easier to use. Digital cameras are now comparably priced with good film cameras and provide a color image, although, at the time of this writing, the quality of the image is poorer than a photograph. These electronically stored images can be called up along with the catalogue records and give your audience access to the collection without having to handle the objects.

Remember that electronically stored data do not have an infinite shelf life—in fact, it is relatively short—while a properly made and stored photograph has a long life. It may be very difficult to convert an image from one program to another, although a majority of programs will read most of the imaging conventions. However, CD-ROM disks may be more permanent than even a photograph on good paper, so long as there are hardware and software to read them. An ideal arrangement might be to have both a photograph and an electronic image. As the technology develops, you may be able to do both with one camera.

Videotape

A videotape of the collection would be a good documentation of the inventory. Videotape would be an excellent record as a beginning in a badly catalogued collection. As in any other electronic medium, videotape will deteriorate over time and the technology changes. It must be rerecorded periodically to preserve it. Videotape has an advantage over movie film (which does not have a long shelf life either) in that you can make it under light conditions that would forbid the use of film.

The Physical Catalogue

You can get cards from library supply houses. I favor a larger card, such as 4 x 6 inches, which holds a great deal more information than the standard 3 x 5 inch card. However, they are harder to find in the right card stock and it is difficult to get file cabinets for them. The ubiquitous 3 by 5″ card is readily available, and the file cabinets for them are obtainable from many sources. Since card file cabinets get a great deal of use, they should be of good quality.

When every card had to be typed by hand, typing them on good card stock made sense because you expected the card to last forever. Now that even the smallest museum will have access to a word processor, a cheaper stock might be used. As records are updated the old cards are thrown out and new ones generated. Some museums generate a whole new card catalogue periodically, and archive the old one.

Each object should have its own card, even when there are numerous identical examples of the same object, such as a set of dishes. It helps when you have to deal with just one of these similar objects.

Even a small museum will need a large number of cards. Printing a form on them can be expensive. For this reason, I recommend that only one type of card be printed, although it is possible to place all the information on a blank card. This is the Main Entry Card. You can use the same card form for several different types of catalogues.

Typing catalogue cards is a real chore. Any step you can take to reduce the work is worth the effort. It is a good idea to arrange the data on the Worksheet (C-4) in the same order that it is typed on the cards. This will promote accuracy as well as speed up the process. You can also buy almost any size card in a continuous strip that will fit most typewriters or printers. Most data managers are able to print forms and cards or to send data to a form created in a word processor. This can be configured in any form you find useful. Some people do not use a computer but type catalogue cards into a word processor. If you can type all those records into a word processor, why can't you type them into a data management program? The cost for either program is about the same.

Catalogues Without Cards

There are catalogues without cards. One kind is a computer catalogue. Some museums have very static collections or static exhibits. In such cases, it is often easier to list the information on sheets of paper. These "page catalogues" are kept in file drawers or loose-leaf binders and can easily be copied on any office copier. The big disadvantage is that a change in any item affects the whole catalogue.

I have discussed paper catalogues chiefly in terms of cards. The advantage of cards over lists on paper is that cards can be easily shuffled and a change on one card does not affect the whole list.

Computer Catalogues

You need the same kind of information from a computer catalogue that you need from a card file. There should be some assurance that your program can extract the information you want and present it in usable form on both screen and paper. These reports are substitutes for the old paper catalogues. Most data management programs can be made to configure almost any kind of report using the data in its data bank.

You must be able to access the information you need. You might wish to generate a list of all the silver in storage, which would make searches much easier. You might have the list sorted by accession number, location, donor, and title. These will do very well as catalogues. The advantage in this is that you can often take the whole catalogue (or the computer itself) with you when you go out into the collection. The corrected data can be entered into your computer every so often, and this will keep the master record complete and accurate. If you want them, the computer can just as easily be made to generate cards.

Again, the size of the collection plays a part as to whether you generate paper catalogues from the computer. It a lot easier for a small collection to have a printout than a large one. Generating 3,000 cards with the typical office printer may be more than a day's work; generating 100,000 may take more than a month. Even simple reports, where each record takes up only one line, can be quite extensive. A complete report of one line of data for each record for a collection of 10,000 objects might take up over 200 pages. Still, that is less than the seven or so drawers a card catalogue of the same size collection might use. Most museums with a data bank, if they generate paper records at all, use them for specific tasks, such as inventory, and use the computer for cataloguing.

I discuss computers in Chapter Eight. For now, you should make sure that the program can edit, sort, index or otherwise compile the information you need from your record and present it in some usable form.

Inventories

The inventory is used to check the accuracy of the information you have on each object, its condition, and its location. Catalogues will stay up-to-date only if there is an periodic inventory. The ideal is to inventory your collection once a year. This may be beyond the capabilities of a small museum, but if you do about a third of the museum each year you will have examined the whole collection every three years. I would bet the mortgage that any collection that has not been inventoried in the last three years has numerous problems with its registration system.[9]

The large collection poses a problem. A collection of 10,000 objects may take two teams several days to inventory, but what about a collection of 100,000 objects? In this situation, it may be necessary to take a "spot" inventory. This inventory only looks at a small portion of the collection to see if there are problems.

You might take 100 records at random and see if you can find the objects and see if their records are up to date. Then pick 100 objects from several storage areas and examine their records. If there are few problems this will give you an idea of the state of the collection, but it is not a complete inventory and any problems lurking below the surface may stay undiscovered for a long while.

For manual systems, many museums inventory by making a list of the objects as they find them and checking that list against the records (see C-8). That list becomes an accurate record of the state of the collection at that particular time. There is, however, a lot of cross checking of records.

As you go through the collection, you may find it easier to take one of your card catalogues and move the card for each object you find to a *found* file. This method does not produce a list, so you will have to make one from the completed catalogue. I use this method and create a list as I go along.

It is a lot easier inventorying a computerized collection. You generate a list of the objects by location and check them off as you find them, or you can take the computer with you, if it is small enough.

It is important with inventories that you end up with some list showing the state of the collection at that particular time. This list should be archived.

Certain new devices may have a profound effect on inventorying the collection in the future. Barcode readers are one such device. The technology is well developed, reliable, and relatively cheap.[10] Right now, they are used very much like those in a supermarket. One reads the barcode for the location and the computer reads each object at that location. There are safe ways to place the barcodes on most objects using paper tags. This type of technology is developing and may become a must.

An inventory requires a large commitment on the part of the museum. Make sure you can complete it before you start. One of the curses of badly registered systems is all the incomplete inventories that one has to deal with.

Access

How much of the museum's records are public documents is a question you should consider carefully. Most museums do not consider any of the registration records public information. In most cases access is restricted to only a few of the museum personnel. This practice is a sensible one. Any data made public are carefully edited before release. Remember, labels, exhibit catalogues, education programs, and similar published information are public releases of information about your catalogue.

Many museum have *portions* of their catalogue easily available to the public through a computer, or even have it on the Internet. This gives the public access without endangering the records or revealing any secrets.

If the museum catalogue is considered a public document, there should be some restrictions on how it is used by the public. Locations and valuations should be privileged information. Privacy laws restrict the use of donors' names and addresses. Knowledge about the size of certain holdings may make you a juicy target for thieves.

Catalogues bring up the question of access, not only to the museum records, but the collection as well. The museum has to grant everyone equal access to the collection. This does not mean that you have to admit everyone any time they want, but you have to let people under similar circumstances have *equal* access. It is a good idea to develop a policy on access to the records and the collection. Access can be limited to legitimate research goals and a need-to-know basis. The type of examination can be restricted to certain times and methods of examination. You can forbid the handling of the object, if that is in its best interest.[11]

Examination of records can be limited to the catalogue. You can keep some data confidential such as the value, location, and the donor's name. Government-run museums may come under so-called sunshine laws, by which they have to grant anyone access to the collection. Access doesn't necessarily have to be to the records. You may have to give someone a list of your Chinese teapots, but that doesn't mean you must give them the whole catalogue. Even then, certain knowledge such as donor's names and the location and value of objects can be restricted, and need-to-know questions may arise. Your lawyer can advise you on this. I have placed a clause on access to the collection in the policy manuals in the appendix.

What Not to Do and When Not to Do It

A mistake people often make about a card catalogue is to confuse it with the accession records. It is tempting to type all the accession records on cards, neatly file them in some fashion, and say you have a catalogue. It is equally easy to take a card from the file and lose it or misplace it, and then you have lost one of the primary records of the museum. This was true of all the problem collections with which I have dealt. If you are going to have a catalogue, keep it separate from the primary records. The catalogue gets used and will eventually have to be replaced, but the primary records should last forever.

I realize that if the museum uses the ledger as their catalogue they could eventually wear it out. In this case, I recommend that the museum make a copy and use the copy instead of the original. In fact, you should copy any primary record that is going to be consulted frequently and use the copy as the working document.

Another mistake is to have a different form for each type of catalogue card. There will be a card for the main entry, another type for the room catalogue, another for the photograph.[12] Unless you have a large printing budget and lots of people to shuffle cards, it is better to keep the number of cards to a minimum. The card you use for your main entry can serve for most other cross references. The donor, association, and lexicon cards can be typed on blank stock. One way to separate one type of card from another is to use different colored stock. There are examples of catalogue cards in the appendix (C-7).

There is a trick to cataloguing. The trick is to do it right the first time. It is a common mistake when cataloguing to start off on the wrong foot, do half a job, drop it, come back later, and start again. The result is a mess. It is better to decide at the beginning what you really want to do, begin it carefully, and complete one section before going on to the next.

Conclusion

Cataloguing is as much a process as it is a device. The process is a constant updating of the data on the collection. This is the way we pass our knowledge on to the next set of curators. There should be a commitment on the part of the museum to updating the catalogue.

The test of a catalogue is not whether you can use it, but whether anyone else can. It should be arranged so it makes sense to anyone. Good cataloguing consists of:

1. Examining every object and every record and resolving any conflicts between the two.
2. Developing a usable set of categories for searches you will actually make.
3. Developing a program to keep the data up to date.

For paper catalogues the purpose of cataloguing is to arrange your records in usable categories. It is easier to shuffle cards than objects. Museum personnel should decide what information will be needed from the catalogue and then divide the catalogue into those units. There may be other methods of cataloguing available that do not use cards. The museum must be careful not to create a catalogue monster that will eat up all the professional staff's time.

A computerized catalogue should be able to quickly and easily provide the information you need in a usable form. Like the card catalogue, the system should be usable to any intelligent person, though he or she may have to learn the idiosyncrasies of the program first when questions of data security arise.

Once the catalogue is created, it should be used in preference to the primary records.

NOTES

1. The term may be correctly spelled either "catalog" or "catalogue." I prefer the latter and was convinced of its utility after two hours in a bar with a Canadian friend, who explained that "cataloging" just could not be pronounced correctly. It seemed like a reasonable argument at the time.

2. Dudley and Wilkinson have a great deal of practical information about cataloguing scattered throughout the book; for history museums see Pearsall, *op. cit.* It would be an interesting subject, but for some reason or another, no one has ever treated cataloguing of museum objects in a book-length treatise.

3. The question of who had the first museum registration system is moot. Herodotus implies, in the fifth century BC that there were catalogues for the collections in the several treasuries (that held historical collections) at Delphi and Mesopotamia. This information may have been oral, but at least the priests could account for their collections and pass this knowledge on. Some of the information was written directly on the object. This is a method frowned on today, but one must say it would be hard to lose your catalogue. Earlier, some of the cities of the ancient world often had what we would call historical collections as part of their temples and treasuries. They had a method of preserving the historical record, but this may also have been an oral record, a system not completely absent today. The concept of a collection ledger was developed in Hellenistic times (350–0 BC). For a survey, see Geoffrey D. Lewis, "Collections, Collectors and Museums: A Brief World Survey," Thompson, *Museum Curatorship, op. cit.,* pp. 7–22.

4. Robert G. Chenhall, *The Revised Nomenclature for Museum Cataloging: A Revised and Expanded Version of Robert G. Chenhall's System for Classifying Man-Made Objects.* Revised and expanded by James R. Blackaby, Patricia Greeno, and the Nomenclature Committee (AltaMira Press, Walnut Creek, CA, 1996). It is interesting, but Chenhall's work, originally meant to aid in the computerization of collections, has proven even more useful with manual records.

5. The only one we are going to consider is Toni Peterson, Director, *Art and Architecture Thesaurus,* 2nd ed. (New York: Oxford University Press, 1994). AAT is also published on disk and will fit many computer programs. The necessity to have a classification constant may need some consideration as the computer industry develops software capable of easily making very sophisticated searches. The computer can develop its own classes of data, but it is easier if there is one built into the system. For a list of all the data standards, see http://www.cidoc.icom.org/stand2.htm. For some reason, Chenhall's system is not on this list.

6. A taxonomy is the classification of a something into a natural arrangement. The list itself is a taxis. Lexicon, nomenclature, and dictionary are more or less interchangeable terms.

7. The reason for placing the name of the museum at the bottom is that it will identify the card, while the important information is at the top.

8. The negative number in this instance is the date that the negative was taken, the first shot on the first roll on March 8, 1977. This is a handy way to keep track of such things.

9. Judith A. Brundin et al., "Inventorying A Historic Property," *Museum News,* 63, 1 (October 1984), pp. 17–25; Pullen, *op. cit.*

10. Catherine Zwiesler, "Barcoding," *Spectra,* 23, 1 (Fall 1995), pp. 18–20, discusses use of barcodes at the National Museum of Natural History. *Spectra* is the newsletter of the Museum Computer Network.

11. Access to the museum collection and the records has not been a very big issue until now. It is the kind of situation people worry about before it happens. However, it is good to be prepared. Malaro, *Primer*, pp. 51, 293–294; Roland W. Force, "Museum Collections: Access, Use and Control," *Curator*, 18, 4 (December 1975), pp. 249–255; Jeanette A. Richoux, Jill Serota-Braden, and Nancy Demyttenaere, "A Policy for Collection Access," *Museum News*, 59, 7 (July/August, 1981), pp. 43–47.

12. As an example, Blackaby et al., *Special Report #3, op. cit.*, shows *seven* different cards with eight sides). For my typical museum of 10,000 objects, this would be 70,000 cards!

Seven

Loans

Unless the exhibits and the collection are very static, a museum will lend and borrow objects. The museum will find that its collection is never complete enough to make up every exhibit. It is good museum practice and good public relations to have exhibits of items from the community. Other museums and organizations will want to tap your resources. Items are often lent or borrowed for purposes of study or conservation. The sophisticated handling of loans is part of the registration process. Like any other part of the registration process, the museum should decide how deeply it wants to get into loans, create the policy to do this, and the procedures will develop out of this.[1]

Loan Policy

Many problems with loans will never occur if the museum has a strong policy on loans. The policy should assure that:

- The loan furthers the purpose of the museum. If your statement of purpose declares that the museum wishes "to encourage the preservation and study of Hero County history," then the loan should do just that.
- The object will be cared for properly while on loan.
- The registration system can track the object over the whole period of the loan even if that is several years!

Every loan should be tested against these conditions. There is an example of such a policy in both Appendices A and B.

There is a difference between things a museum borrows and things it lends, so we are going to discuss these separately. As in any other contractual relationship between a museum and second parties, the loan policies, the loan form, and the types of liability assumed should be gone over carefully with a lawyer before the museum becomes involved in loans.

Loans from the Museum

When a museum lends items out from its collection it is very simple. The museum owns the object lent and can set its own conditions. The museum can have absolute control over how the object is used. Criteria for conditions for loans from the museum are below and in the appendix (C-9).

Loans to the Museum

You are on slightly different ground when you borrow something than when you lend. When you lend, the object involved is your property and you can set the conditions. When you borrow, it is not your property, you must follow the owner's wishes, and you take on a liability. You are obligated to return the loaned object in the same condition in which you received it. You are responsible for it as long as you have it. If the owner does not show up to reclaim it, you are still responsible for it. If the lender appears thirty-three years later, as happened to me once, you are still responsible. Therefore, it is a very good idea to borrow only for specific purposes, such as display, and for a specific time period, and to return things as soon as possible.

For loans to the museum, you must usually provide the protection, shipping, and insurance. Most museums agree to protect the item as if it were their own and to carry fine arts insurance. The owner may want to set other conditions, and these should be stated on the form. Criteria for conditions for a loan to the museum are below and in the appendix (C-10).

Conditions of Loans

The general conditions affecting every loan should printed on the loan form and discussed with the other parties. If there will be special conditions that are not on the loan form, these should then be made a written part of the loan documents. Before the object is moved the loan form should be signed by all parties.

Whether the loan is from or to the museum certain conditions arise that should be accounted for in the museum's policy and loan arrangements. These are:

Whose Loan Procedures Will Apply?

As a practical matter, there should only be one loan agreement. On loans between museums, the lending institution will have the upper hand, and it will almost always be their procedure and forms that are used. This can be pretty tricky when the museums vary widely in operating procedures. On third-party loans, that is loans for traveling exhibits, the policies of the originating museum will probably apply. Your loan form is for people who normally do not have their own form, such as individuals and private companies.

What Is Actually Being Borrowed?

The loan form should state exactly what is being borrowed. On loans from your museum your accession records are very handy, as you can place the accession number and a description from your records on the loan form. On loans to the museum you may have to go to the lending person or agency and make an exact description of what is borrowed and a condition report.

The description of the object should be good enough to identify it in court. The museum's description of its own objects should do that. If the description of a borrowed item is not good enough, you will have to make a new one. When borrowing from a private person you should go over the description and make sure the lender agrees with your description particularly of condition.

The Exact Purpose of the Loan

The purpose of the loan should be stated on the form. If you lend a copper pot for exhibit you do not want to see it used for cooking. It is best for the museum to have a policy on why they are involved in loans. Many museums simplify the arrangement by developing a policy that they will only borrow objects for exhibit in the museum, and only lend objects to other museums for the same purpose. Museums with a local following may find it expedient to lend to community organizations that are able to take care of the object. In addition, there should be some way to lend objects for conservation or study.

How the Object Is to Be Cared for and Handled while on Loan

It is very important to understand exactly how the object is to be handled while on exhibit. That means if it is to be exhibited only, how much, if any, access anyone is to have to it during the loan? Also, what happens to it before it reaches its final destination? Is the janitor going to unpack it or the curator? Where it is going to be stored en route? Who is going to handle it while on exhibit and how? Who is going to pack it when the loan period is up? These are typical but important considerations.

Normally, the borrowers' care of the object is limited to simple dusting, although even that may not be allowed for certain objects. The other party should notify the lender of any change in the condition of the object and be forbidden to make repairs in the case of damage. How the object is to be cased, lighted, protected, and other environmental concerns are all conditions that should be agreed upon in advance.

If the object requires special handling, should not be in harsh light, must be in controlled humidity, needs special security, etc., these conditions should be gone over step by step with the borrower before the loan is made. It is a good idea to go over all the provisions of the loan before the loan form is signed. One thing you should know is if the donor wants their name advertised in another location.

An Assessment of the Object's Condition and Ability to Travel and Withstand the Conditions It Will Be Under during the Loan

Any details of condition should be noted before the object is sent out. The condition should be the same when it is brought back. You should have a Condition Report (appendix, C-12) on each object in the loan, whether from or to the museum, and have both parties agree on the statements on this form. You may need two condition reports or have to update the original; once when the object is lent, and once when it is returned. If you are borrowing an object, and there is no condition report by the lender, then that should be noted. You should demand that you make a condition report at the time of the receipt and that this be the condition of record. Otherwise, the borrower may claim you caused old damage.

Condition reports should not only be made out when the object is loaned, but whenever it is examined. Ideally, there should be at least one condition report on each object in the collection. As the object is monitored, there will be a number of condition reports if there are changes in the condition.

The condition of the building that houses the object is also a consideration. Many museums have a facility report that they use for loans to other agencies. There is a standard form developed by the Registrars Committee of AAM.[2] Filling in the facilities report is a time-consuming thing, but only has to be done once and then can be used with any other loan.

An object may be in good enough condition to be exhibited in one place, but in too fragile a condition to be exhibited in another. An assessment of the object's ability to travel is an important part of the loan process. Occasionally, if the other party really has to have this object, they will pay for the conservation necessary (or at least share the cost) to have the object travel.

Method of Packing or Crating

How the object is to be packed for shipping, and who will do it, are important questions. For many objects, packing as for a typical move of household goods, may be enough. for many other objects, specialized packing or crating may be required, and climate control may even be necessary. This has to be done both ways. How this is done and who will pack and unpack should be part of the loan agreement.

Method of Transporting the Object and Who Is Responsible for the Shipment

There is a museum in western Pennsylvania where board members were expected to move objects. They once had a provision that to become a board member you had to have a pickup truck. That may work with agricultural equipment but it will not work in most museums.

Make sure that both borrower and lender know how the object is to be transferred and who is responsible for the transfer. Is it going to be the curator, a courier, a trucking company, a local moving company, or an expert in transporting fine arts? The borrower is usually responsible for making the arrangements and paying for the move. These conditions should be approved by the other party. When lending objects, be certain that the borrower will move the equipment, personnel, and object with sufficient care, *both* ways.

The problem you sometimes run into with loans is where the other party will be located at the end of the loan term. If you borrow an object from a lender who is located 10 miles away, then the costs and problems of the move are very clear. But what happens if that same person moves 3,000 miles away during the loan period? This situation does not just apply to individuals but can happen to museums as well. It is best to specify that the costs of the move only apply to shipment to the address on the loan form.

What happens if the owner sells or transfers the property while it is on loan is also a consideration. They should notify you in writing if this occurs. You should normally not return an object to anyone but the person who signed the loan form as the owner. If it is transferred, it is the owner's responsibility to provide proof of the transfer, not the museum's.

Museums often have problems of not being able to return an object when the loan period is up. The owner, for one reason or another, is not available to take it back. The museum should require that, if they cannot return the object because the owner cannot receive it, the museum can then exercise a lower standard of care, or even charge rent. In some states, it is possible that the object could eventually become the museum's property. Most museums, however, may be required to keep the property indefinitely until a legitimate owner is ready to receive it. In the case of the death of the owner, the museum may have to keep the object until the estate is settled. This can run to years.

All the Locations in which the Loan Will Be

The exact route the object is to be taken to its final destination, and where it will rest en route, should be agreed upon. I once had a very valuable object left untended in the middle of a busy mall by someone who I thought was a responsible borrower. It was lucky that I happened along to rescue it.

It is best if the borrower keeps the object in their possession and returns it to the museum when the term of the loan is completed. Sometimes there is a reason to lend it to a third party. A good example would be a museum making up a traveling exhibition from the collections of several museums.

The Exact Dates of the Loan Period,
Wall to Wall

The date of the loan period should include the date the agreement is made, the date the object is to be picked up, the dates of the exhibit (if the object is lent for that purpose), and the date it is to be returned. There should never be any confusion about loan dates.

Almost all loans are made "wall-to-wall." That means the borrower is responsible for the object from the time it is first handled to prepare it to be moved until it is returned to that same place, or a time mutually agreeable to both parties. Thus, the borrower's responsibility begins once anyone lays their hand on the loaned object while it is still in the owner's building.

There are "door-to-door" agreements, in which the borrower is only responsible for the object after it leaves the lender's door until it is returned there. These are not popular any more, as the preparation of the object for transport is now considered part of the loan process. If you do not specify that the loan is wall-to-wall, then the loan would probably be considered door-to-door.

The loan should have definite time limits. A loan to the museum should not continue for a long period of time; a year is long enough and three years are about the maximum. Occasionally, museums borrow for longer periods of time. One should hesitate to request an unusually long time period, but sometimes there is a good reason: it may be the only way some rare item can be exhibited or the owner may not have clear title just yet. These long-term loans should be for a period of a year or two, renewable from year to year. This practice will remind both parties that it is still a loan and it will remind you to keep up your fine arts insurance. The number of these long-term loans should be kept to a minimum.

The Value of Each Object in the Loan

The value of the object is a very complicated thing when insurance is involved. If you have a damaged object that is worth $1,000 and the repairs costs $1,500, who is responsible for the difference? The insurance company may pay the $1,000 and then take the object for its salvage value. The owners may only get $800 or so if they keep the object. What happens if one of a set gets destroyed? Overvaluing an object to take care of some of this may not work as the insurance company usually will only insure a "fair market value." Emotional value is usually not insurable. The museum should agree that it is only responsible for the declared value and make sure that value is reasonable for the object.

Each object in the loan should have its own value. This is important as damage or theft to the whole loan will practically never come up, but damage to a single piece will be an occasional occurrence. Sometimes the museum will have exhibits of items collected from the community, such as a senior citizens art fair. It may be impossible to evaluate each object, but you can give a range of values, $X to $XXX, that will cover the whole loan.

The museum should be careful about offering to value objects lent to it. This may place the museum in the position of evaluating the object for market. If something happens and the value is incorrect, it may place the museum in a bad legal position. The owner might claim damages. If there is a problem with this, you may have to hire an appraiser. Who pays for this is an interesting question.

The Type and Nature of the Insurance and Who Is Responsible for Paying for It

The usual practice is for the borrower to be responsible for the insurance. It is important to have proof of insurance. There is a form any insurance agent should be able to produce called a "Certificate of Insurance." When borrowing, make sure that the insurance is not due to expire while the object is on loan. The expiration date will usually be on the certificate of insurance. It's useful to have a 120-day cancellation clause on these certificates of insurance. For objects of small value, where the borrower is well known, the museum may waive the demand for insurance. The lender really does not want the money, they want the object back in the same condition you lent it.[3]

The Name and Signature of the Person Actually Responsible for the Loan

If the person borrowing the object represents the organization, he or she should be responsible enough to place his or her organization under the obligation of caring for the object.

The person who signs for the loan should the one who is really responsible for it, not the person who picks it up. These are often two different people. The person who picks up the object should also sign, but may not be the responsible person.

This can be one of the tricky parts of loan arrangements. The organization responsible for the object may not be located at the museum or even in the same city (or state) as the exhibiting organization. It is important to get the name of a responsible person and the exact address of everyone involved. If there is a parent organization, it might be a good idea to find out if it knows that its satellite museum is borrowing the object. Museums may have different street addresses for the offices, the exhibit hall, and the shipping dock. Get them all.

Request for the Return of the Loan before the Loan Period Is Up

It is not unknown for an owner to request the return of the object before the loan period is up. That may leave a big hole in your exhibit. Common practice is to allow this, but to require a thirty- or sixty-day notice before exercising this right. It is customary to have the person requesting the early return of the loan pay the packing and shipping fees.

Control of Intellectual Property

The intellectual property of the museum consists of such things as the images of the objects in the collection, the content and appearance of documents, the content and methods of education programs, publications, etc. If the appearance of the buildings or site of the museum is part of the "signature" of the museum, that, too, is intellectual property. Museums were pretty careless with their intellectual property until recently. With the advent of sophisticated communication devices, this intellectual property suddenly has a real value to the museum. Steps should be made to protect it, particularly while on loan.

Although the object itself may be in the public domain, a photographic or electronic image of it may be copyrighted. Museums should exercise control over who takes these images and what purpose they are used for. Before you allow anyone to photograph or otherwise copy anything in the museum, you should restrict its use to a certain time period and to certain uses (e.g., "A one-time use in a book on left-handed monkey wrenches."). While the object is on loan to another institution, you may want to restrict their right to photograph the object only for record-keeping purposes or for a catalogue.

The new forms of electronic imagery are so sophisticated that any use has to be carefully circumscribed or you can lose all control over the image of an object in your collection. This has applied mainly to art works in the past, but one should guard all intellectual property. I have clauses in my loan forms that restrict use of images to record shots and a one-time use in a catalogue.

Amending the Loan Agreement

You should guard against oral amendments to the loan agreement. It is too easy to have a misunderstanding. There should be a clause that the agreement may only be amended in writing and must be signed by both parties.

Loan Numbers and a Loan Register

Museums that borrow a lot of material often keep a loan register and assign numbers to each borrowed item. This is a good idea if you are mounting four or six large loan exhibits a year or have a large turnover in loans. Loan registers are normally kept only for loans to the museum. You already have a record of your own objects, and the loan register gives you control over all the objects in the museum that are not part of your collection. Some museums also keep a register of objects loaned from the museum, but I do not think that is necessary, unless you have an inordinate number of them. Loan numbers were discussed in Chapter Three, but are only assigned to the items you borrow; your own objects have accession numbers. A loan register might look like the example in the appendix (C-13).[4] The loan register should be checked periodically and the status of all loans cleared. At the end of the year, the register and all loans should be up to date and the status of all loans reported to the board.

I am only suggesting a loan register, as it is an excellent device to keep track of loans, if you have a number of them during the year. I doubt it would be necessary if you make fewer than five or so such transactions a year. Whether a loan register would be helpful depends on the staff and the time you have available. Keeping all the current loan forms in a file is another way of tracking them.

Unless you have some way of entering objects on loan to the museum into your computer, a loan register may be necessary with that device as well. If the museum borrows only a few objects a year, I would think that creating a computer record on them is a lot of work. If you have a large number of loans to the museum, you may find such a record necessary. There are things called "flags" in many computer programs. These allow you to tag certain records with a number or letter. Flagging objects is a good way of tracking all loans from the museum.

Conservation Loans

Museums often lend or borrow things for conservation or identification. These transactions are handled pretty much as any other loan. When the museum lends out an object to be conserved, the administration should have a pretty good idea what the conservator is going to do with it. The conservator should look at the object before borrowing it and then state in writing what he or she proposes to do. If this is impossible, the object is sent to the conservator for examination first. The conservator will then report back on the proposed treatment. If that is agreeable, the recommendation is made part of the loan form. The loan agreement should be loose enough to allow the conservator some room to work if he or she runs into problems and tight enough to prevent him or her from doing more than the museum staff wishes. The time limits have to be somewhat looser on these loans as the conservator will often run into problems, and you do not want to rush the conservator, but there should be a finite time limit. Loans can always be extended.

The museum or its staff will sometimes do conservation work for outsiders. When that is done, the transaction becomes a business deal and not a museum function. The museum should have the protections that any business has, particularly liability. One of the ways to justify the cost of a conservation laboratory is the ability to use the excess capacity of the lab for outside work. In these instances, the museum should be as strict on its procedure on the items it takes in as if it were borrowing any other item.

Deposit or "Drop-Off" Loans

If someone leaves an object at the museum, even without the knowledge or permission of the museum, that object is very likely the museum's responsibility until it is returned. There are also loans pending gift giving or similar temporary loans. For these reasons, it is best to have a policy about what is to be received at the museum. This is especially important with volunteer-run museums, where there may be a large number of people working at the reception area of the museum over the course of the year. It might be best to have a simple statement such as the example placed where every volunteer can see it:

> If anyone brings in an object with the offer to donate, sell, or lend it to the Hero County Historical Society, the object may not be accepted or left at the museum without the permission of Mrs. Supreme Optimist, 728–2208, or Mrs. Usually V. Negative, 266–4500. If they are not available, inform the potential donor that the Society may be interested in their object, but that you may not receive it, and that the potential donor should get in touch with either of those persons.

If permission is granted, then the proper form can be signed so that both parties know their responsibilities.

In instances such as this, the museum may find it useful to have a "deposit" form that allows prospective donors to temporarily leave items at the museum while awaiting acceptance. A deposit form allows the museum to keep the object for a short period of time, pending the preparation of other forms, but does not obligate the museum as deeply as a loan form or gift agreement might. A sample deposit form is in the appendix (C-11).

People will often bring things to the museum for identification. It is a good practice to have a policy on this. I recommend not doing it at all. If the museum accepts an object for identification, it is a loan just as much as any other loan. It should be treated accordingly. If the museum receives no real benefit from the loan, there is a question whether it should be accepted at all. Some museums have a separate form for identification or conservation loans, but I don't think it is necessary.

There is a small historical society to which someone once offered to give 25,000 sea shells (all different), weighing 2 1/2 tons. Only chance kept the shells from being left. A procedure such as outlined above can prevent embarrassment.

Existing Long-Term Loans

There is no such thing as a permanent loan; it is either a loan or it is not. Lawyers have a fascinating language. I used to play bridge with two of them and asked them to research our legal liabilities with regard to loans. One came up with the fact that a loan was a "gratuitous bailment without the right of survivorship." I liked that. Both agreed that a loan never becomes the museum's property, no matter how long it is kept, though that situation has been changed in certain states. As I have pointed out, there may be a good reason to take in a long-term loan, but never kid yourself that it is yours. It is best to have such loans on a one- or two-year basis, and then neither party will forget the status of the property.

Laws vary widely, and there may be some way of claiming legal title. Almost half the states have passed laws that allows the museum to acquire title to permanent loans.[5]

For everyone else, acquiring title to long-term loans is difficult, at best, and is always subject to question if the owner or heirs appear. In one case with which I am familiar, the heirs showed up more than ninety years later. Only the fact that there were twenty heirs and they could not agree on who got the objects kept the items in the museum. Even under such circumstances, such objects are not the museum's, nor will they ever be, under the present laws of that state.[6]

The best method of clearing such loans is to attempt to track down the original lenders or their heirs and to try to get them to donate the objects or to claim them. That is a time-consuming and unpleasant task, but it may be necessary.[7] When you try to clear up long-term loans, you often risk losing a valuable object, but that is better than offering free storage.

What Not to Do and When Not to Do It

Do not fail to get everything in writing. Loans are usually made to people with whom the museum is acquainted. There is a tendency to be a bit careless on procedure when the object has no great value or the deal is between friends. If you have a loan procedure, it is a good idea to stick to it. If any questions come up, you will have the details in writing.

Many things about loans that should not be done fall into the curatorial area rather than the area of registration, and so are outside the scope of this book. The person making the loan must ensure that the object will be taken care of when it is out of the museum and that the loan will not bring discredit to the museum. For that reason, I am always leery of loans for promotional purposes. You never know, if you lend a carriage to an automobile dealer for promotion, that you will not see it prominently displayed in all the media with a caption, "Look at this stupid, creaky old carriage that we got from the musty old historical society. Why drive this when you can drive a Total?"[8] It is wise to make sure that any prospective borrower who is unknown to you is actually who the say they are and really represents the organization they claim to represent. We usually insist that the borrower writes to us on the organization's stationary, stating what is wanted to borrow and how they intend to display it.

Loans to the museum tend to be carefully made and cared for until the exhibit is over, then the pressure is off and you may get a little careless. That loan is your baby until the owner has it in hand and is satisfied with its condition. Do not relax your care a minute.

Conclusion

When a museum borrows or lends an object, it places its reputation on the line. A carefully thought-out loan procedure will prevent most problems. Remember, in 999 cases out of 1,000 things go well. The one time there is a problem is the one that causes all the trouble. The loan policy of the museum should be such that it handles the 999 cases well and has all its homework done for the one problem case.

NOTES

1. Malaro, *Primer*, pp. 156–234, has an extensive discussion of the legal aspects of loans. Phelan, *Guide*, pp. 107–108, has a more limited discussion of loans but in her *Museum Law*, pp. 273–277, there is an extensive discussion from the lawyer's viewpoint; Gallery Association of New York, *Insurance and Risk Management for Museums and Historical Societies* (Hamilton, NY: Gallery Association, 1986) is an excellent handbook. Loans, as a practical, rather than a legal matter, are discussed in Dudley and Wilkinson, pp. 89–137, and *passim*; AAM Registrar's Committee, professional Practices Subcommittee, "Loan Survey Report," May 1990 reported some interesting things. One was that 21 percent of history museums did not have a loan policy. You can see what the unwritten standards are by looking at this report.

2. AAM Registrars' Committee, *Standard Facility Report*, Professional Practice Series, AAM Technical Service (Washington, DC: AAM, 1989).

3. Gallery Associates, *op. cit.*; Dudley and Wilkinson, pp. 139–154, has a very useful chapter on insurance.

4. The loan number is optional. For a discussion of loan numbers see Dudley and Wilkinson, pp. 27–28.

5. There is discussion of various remedies for long-term loans with state-by-state legislation current at the time by Linden Havemeyer, "Old Loans: A Collections Management Problem," *Registrar*, 8, 2 (Fall 1991), pp. 25–39.

6. Malaro, *Primer*, pp. 165–167 and 178–179 has an excellent discussion of "permanent loans." A good procedure for it has been set out in Anita Manning, "Converting Loans to Gifts," *AASLH Technical Leaflet #94* (Nashville: AASLH, 1977); Phelan, *Museum Law*, p. 108, notes that there are two types of gratuitous bailments depending on the "benefit" one gets from the loan; Malaro, *Primer*, 195–203.

7. AAM, "The High Cost of a Permanent Loan," *Museum News*, 66, 4 (February 1988), p. 38.

8. Be aware that you may be creating a precedent when you lend objects to commercial or noneducational agencies, which may force you to lend museum items to agencies or for purposes which you would rather not; Malaro, *Primer*, pp. 174–175. But Malaro does not know of a single instance where this has occurred. She just warns you that the possibility exists.

Eight

Computers

A computer can do a lot of good things for your registration system, but it is just a machine, and like any other machine, you have to have the right one for the job.[1] I am going to suggest an approach to computers that will fit the small museum. I will assume that the reader knows enough about computers to make intelligent choices, or can acquire this information. I can't be too specific in this chapter as the technology changes too quickly. If I get too technical, the advice will be obsolete before this is published.

First Steps

Many failures in using computers result from poor planning. You have to know what you really need before you buy anything. The first thing you should do is make a needs assessment of your museum. The people involved in the collection should get together and develop a list of things they would like to get from the registration system. An analysis of actual searches for information is helpful. In looking at these you begin to understand where to look for information and what to look for. A step-by-step analysis of the most common processes, such as accessioning, loans, catalogue searches for exhibits, updating catalogues, donor requests, inventories, etc., is useful.[2] The lists show you who needs to know what, how much they need to know, in what form the information should be, and how often the information is needed. Just as importantly, they show what information you don't need. An example of a simple analysis of a record search is shown in Figure 16.

A look at your policies and procedures is in order. Do your current records reflect museum policy? A electronic data bank will certainly affect policy. You may no longer need all the paper forms you used to have. Who has access to the data bank is an important question, so you will need new security procedures.

After you take these factors into account, you are ready to start making up a list of fields you want to include. A field is a discrete piece of information, such as the accession number. You can be quite generous when first making up this list of fields. Put in every one you think you will need. The list can (and certainly will) be cut down later. Start thinking about what the field will contain. Should it be only text? Should it be only numbers? How long should it be? These decisions need only be general ideas at this stage, as the type of software you select will have a great deal of bearing on the number and makeup of the fields. A sample list of the fields, recommended by the Common Agenda Data Bases Task Force, is in Chapter Four.

The most important thing to consider is what information you want to get out of the system, as that is the information you must put in. If you are going to require information that is not presently in your records, then you must start thinking about how you are going to acquire it for your new system. For instance, if you do not now track condition, how are you going to find these data and put them in your system? Conversely, if you never look at the date of acquisition, why put it in?[3]

Information That Is Actually Used

When you first see a museum computer system there is often a fascinating variety of screens and data fields. This is all very interesting, but the experience of the museum field is that the more screens and data fields you have, the more difficult it is to enter data into the data bank and access information afterward. You may want a fancy system, but what you really need is a simple system that fits on one or two screens and that will lead you quickly and easily to either the object or the paper record.

Subject of search: "Typical tools on a cabinetmakers workbench."

Actions:	**Analysis:**
Make a list of the tools needed: a bench; types of planes, braces, bits, saws, hammers, clamps, rulers, squares, etc. Sometimes this is done mentally.	Chenhall has a classification for this that would pull all these up at once.
Search catalogue for requisite cards. Search. main entry catalogue. Look through entire tool catalogue. Remove cards as potential objects are found.	The ability to flag, or mark, particular records would be useful so that after the initial search we can find these records again.
List objects by name, number, and location.	The program must be able to generate a report for this purpose.
Search storage for objects.	How are we going to mark location? Should objects "live" at one spot? Shelf lists would be useful.
Return cards to file. Assemble objects in dummy exhibit. Select ones for use.	The flag system has to allow for the objects to be either placed on exhibit or returned to their proper place in storage. If there is need to borrow objects for the exhibit we need ability to account for this.
Set up exhibit.	We need to be able to easily extract information for labels. We need to be able to easily extract donor names for labels. We need to know if there are restrictions on identifying donors. If we are going to track the history of the movement of the object, then we need a record of locations including the exhibit. Need ability to track objects while on exhibit. Orient interpreters, write hand-out literature.Need the ability to pull up information for training purposes. It would be useful to be able to transport catalogue information for labels and training guides.
Take down exhibit.	Need to track objects back to storage.

Figure 16. Analysis of a typical card catalog search.

If you analyze a typical search for useful information in your present system, you will find that you are using only ten or fifteen pieces of data. You seldom have to know if it is painted blue or has astragal ends. What you usually look for is very simple and very specific.

This is the information asked for in most searches of a museum catalogue:[4]

- Accession number
- Title of object ("genus" and "species")
- Classification (after Chenall)
- How acquired (gift, purchase, etc.)
- Source (donor, from whom purchased, etc.)
- Location
- Material
- Size
- Place of origin
- Maker
- Date (of manufacture)
- Description
- Association
- Comment
- Value
- Flag

This record contains most of the information that you will ever need. With some clever manipulation you can get all of these fields on one screen. A record of this length is capable of supporting sophisticated questions such as the location of all silver tea sets with gadrooning made in Boston before 1810 by specific makers.

Accession Number

The numbering field is very important, as that ties the object to the records. If you have two or more numbering systems, an extra field or fields for the other numbering systems is useful. Using these extra number fields, you can utilize some of the old numbering systems when necessary. The computer can also show the relationship between the several numbering systems.

Title and Classification

As we have discussed, these fields are used to identify and classify the object. For reasons of clarity and ease of entry, you need a separate field for the title and the classification.

How Acquired

Using this field, you can separate out the donations from the purchases and other means of acquisition. If you have long-term loans and deaccessions, this field will help identify them. The field need only be one letter long; for example, "L" can stand for "loan." Some museums call this the "status" field.

Source

The source field is a useful field that is used constantly in museums with any number of donations. In the case of purchases, the contributor of the funds is entered, rather than from whom purchased. I list the vendors in the "Comments" field as you seldom need to know who they are.

Location

The best way to indicate location in a computer is to have the object "live" at one location and only track it when it is moved. This is discussed in Chapter Six.

Material

The effectiveness of the material field depends on what the material is. When the object is made mainly of one material, such as glass, silver, tin, or wrought iron, then you will find it a useful way to find or classify certain objects. When there are many materials, such as a chair made of seven different woods, the field will be nearly useless for creating a class, but very useful for identification. It is better to be specific in terminology (for example, "maple" rather than "wood").

Size

The size field is a lot more useful in a computer than it is in a paper catalogue. If you have a separate field for width, height, depth, or diameter, you can extract the number of running feet of objects slated for an exhibit or the cubic volume of the collection. If the size field is to be used in this fashion, dimensions have to be entered decimally. Size fields can be configured to give either inch/foot or metric measurements and can convert one automatically to the other.

Place of Origin

Where the object originated is of great importance as that often influences the style, material, method of construction, or even how the object was used. It is better to be specific (for example, "Boston" rather than "New England"). In some collections, the place of use will be important and you may need a separate field for that as well.

Maker

The "Maker" field is actually the "Creator" field. You should list the artist, engraver, craftsperson, manufacturer, printer as well as publisher, and any other person or entity who had a hand in the construction of the object. If the maker is a school or group (Shakers, U.S. Navy, etc.), that should be indicated here.

Date of Manufacture

The date of manufacture is important, and you have to insist on rigid standards. The computer cannot tell the difference between ca. 1840, c. 1840, about 1840, and 1835–1845. You have to pick one method. I do not like the use of about (ca.) in a computer data bank as it is vague and difficult to access or sort. I prefer to use a range of dates, such as "1770–1800" for either "later 18th century" or "ca. 1784."

Description

Descriptions will be very useful if you can enter all the data. If you have a description field, make sure your program will search it for the data you need. You must be able to perform "string searches" that let you to look for relationships such as all records that contain the words "bow back" and "Windsor." In that fashion you can find all the Windsor chairs with bow backs without having a style field. Instead of separate fields for such things as style or color, include them in the description. This cuts down the number of fields and gives great flexibility in searches.

Association

The computer makes it easier to search for an association of an object with a person, place, or event than a card catalogue. Your program must be able to make "string searches" for useful data, such as the relationship of George Washington with the Whiskey Rebellion. You must have fairly strict rules on how this information is to be entered into the computer if you expect to make any kind of search of this field. It is a time-consuming field to create, but you will use it more than any other.

Comment

A "comment" field is useful for information that is not included in other fields.

Value

Some museums place a value on each object in a collection. You can manipulate this. You can get a total value for the collection or a portion of it, you can upgrade the value if prices rise, or you can get a value for part of the collection. You can determine your risk in certain areas ("the total value of the objects stored in room 101"). You can get a total on a certain class of objects, such as all the silver. Some programs will even round off the values when you raise them a certain percentage.

Flag

A flag field is useful. You can "flag" certain groups of objects that are otherwise unrelated. For instance, you can flag a group of unrelated objects that are to be loaned to another museum and call up their records any time by their flag. This saves calling up each record individually.

Condition

I have not included a condition field, but it would be a useful one if you can track it. Using a simplified ranking method you can establish lists of objects in priority of their need for conservation. You can use this to track condition. A simple system is:

"1" indicates the condition "Urgent." The object needs immediate care.
"2" indicates the condition "Serious but not Urgent." The safety of the object is in jeopardy and its condition will become urgent if handled.
"3" indicates the condition "Requires Treatment." If stored properly, the treatment may be delayed.
"4" indicates the condition "Needs Work." The object may be handled but needs some care. The object may, or may not, be exhibitable.
"5" indicates the condition "Good." The object is exhibitable and requires only maintenance to stay in the present condition.

With this simple priority ranking you can generate reports of your collection's conservation needs.

The Number of Fields

It is very easy to go crazy and have lots and lots of fields. I saw a program once with over 150 fields. I can't imagine what you would do with all of them. You have to keep in mind that the more fields you have, the larger the record and the longer it takes to enter the data, the greater the chance of making errors, the more space that is required in your mass storage devices, the harder it is to back it up, and larger and more expensive equipment is needed. It will also be harder to check for accuracy. Using the sixteen fields above, there would be a potential of 160,000 entries for the 10,000 object collection that I use as an example in this book, but I have seen programs that have a potential for over one million entries for a collection of the same size. I have no idea why you would ever need that many data and how you would maintain such a data bank.

The file for most small museums containing records of the size and nature discussed above would fit into most large microcomputers and could (with several qualifications) be handled by most off-the-shelf data management programs. The entry of data into this record would be *relatively* easy and would take less time than a more extensive record. You have to keep in mind what you are capable of creating and maintaining. A record such as the one proposed is more than adequate for many museums and can always be updated into a larger one.

At this point you are in a better position than you were to evaluate the proposal of some vendor concerning software.

Software

A computer needs a program to tell it what to do. Indeed, it may need several programs to operate. These programs, to a greater or lesser extent, control what you do with your registration system. Programs are called "software." When you wanted to file something with paper records you bought a file cabinet and some folders. You could pretty much dictate how you were going to use these devices, and the technology was easily understood by almost anyone. The operation of computers is not readily apparent to anyone without some study, and software choices are bewildering in their number and complexity.

You should select the software before you select the hardware. The kind of software we will probably be looking at is so-called application software. An application program is the one you use to perform certain structured tasks on the computer such as word processing, spreadsheets, desk-top publishing, and, of course, data management.

The kind of application software that you will probably use for registration is some form of a data management program. These programs will have the ability to create, edit, index, sort data, and display the results on the screen or paper. They will have a report-writing utility built in. They will usually have mail merge ability that allows you to create specialized documents from the data in your collection file with a word processor. This will be part of the ability to import or export the data to or from other programs or applications. As part of the package, the application program may even have a word processor or a spreadsheet utility.

The best-known type of data management program is a "relational data base" program.[5] This kind of program relates each piece of data to every other piece. Not all data managers are relational data bases, but that doesn't mean the ones that are not are not as useful. In fact, you probably won't be able to tell one from the other in operation, and the simpler programs may fit the needs of a small historical museum best. All data managers can be programmed to do specific tasks. How this programming is done is what is important. You will have to analyze the capabilities of the program, particularly the ease of use and, very importantly, the speed with which it operates.

There are many consultants or companies that take other company's software and adapt it to specific situations. They are called Third-Party Vendors, Resellers, or just Vendors, but also Value-Added Dealers or Value-Added Retailers. Almost all your museum-specific computer application programs will come from third-party vendors of one kind or another. There are two choices for you:[6]

- The most easily available is a fully developed collections management application program marketed as a package to the museum field at large. These programs are usually adaptations of existing application programs, but some are written from scratch in one of the available computer languages. I am going to call these "third-party programs." The third-party programs are widely advertised in the professional museum journals, and demonstrated at professional meetings. The opinion of most people I talk to in museums is that most of these programs are adequate and the simpler the program is, the better.
- The other is a program written specifically for you by a third party. These programs are often adaptations of off-the-shelf application programs, but occasionally they are written from scratch in one of the computer languages. I am going to call these "proprietary programs."[7] These proprietary programs are reinventing the wheel, developing a program that has been done many times before, but can give you a program specifically tailored to your needs.

In dealing with vendors, remember this: you are not buying a program, you are buying a registration system! The vendor will be talking about the "program" and you will be talking about the "system." Make sure you are both talking about the same thing!

There are a bewildering number of possibilities and it is difficult enough for an expert to pick the right one, let alone a novice. You will be better able to make a choice if you look at these considerations:

- What do you want the program to do? Is it to be a complete registration system performing all the functions of your old manual registration system? Or is it be an electronic catalogue? If you have made your needs assessment you will be better able to assess this choice. An electronic catalogue will be easier to use and perform most of the tasks you require.

- Does the vendor have a client list? They should. Get the names of nearby museums where this software is installed as much like yours as possible. *Go and look* at the system in operation. There is nothing like an opinion from a user, or several users, to find out how the program really works. If the vendor has never done a museum program, they should be able to supply a list of clients with similar needs as yours.

- Almost all the third-party programs have several screens. A screen is a specific view of a number of the fields in your data bank. You flip from screen to screen looking for specific arrangements of data. Can you easily get to the screen you want or do you have to flip from screen-to-screen-to-screen every time you want to change? Instead of having the vendor demonstrate to you, sit down at the machine and try it yourself! To be useful, these screens require a lot of data entry. Do you need all this information? Can you enter all of it and keep it updated?

- The manuals that come with the various programs are very important. Does the vendor supply you with a manual for their adaptations and can you read and understand it? There will undoubtedly be a manual for the data management program that has been adapted for museum-specific use. Does the vendor supply you with this manual as well? Many programs no longer supply paper manuals and they are contained inside the program. When this is done, check to see if the information is actually useful or just some helpful hint.

- Your data are worthless unless they can be read by a program, so the ability of more than one company's program to read your data is a survival characteristic. In looking at the program that your system is based upon, you are going to have to assess the "portability" of the data that are generated by this program. That is the ability to transfer the data to other programs. The primary reason for this is that programs do not last forever, vendors go out of business, hardware changes, and better programs come along. The other reason is that you may want to use the data in other programs to create useful documents or perform some other function. If you can't make this assessment, then try to get advice from an expert. You have to assume that most widely vended application software are portable, but this is not always true. If in doubt, make the vendor show you that it can!

- You need copies of the disks containing the various programs that actually operates the registration system. Without these disks you cannot make any changes to your program, and perhaps are not able to transport it. Normally, the vendor will give you a package consisting of the program(s), manuals, and anything else that is needed to make it work. But some vendors do not use this method, and you must make sure that you have the "source" programs, or the basic applications, that will interact with your computer, or with others.

Otherwise, you may not be able to alter, upgrade, or transport your program without the vendor—who may not be available, or with whom you may not wish to do business.

- Can the vendor adapt the package specifically for your museum or must you take it as sold? If the vendor can adapt it, is there a fee for this? If it is as sold, is this what you want?

- Is the program written for a history, art, science, or other kind of museum? Many programs are written for art museums and then adapted to other museums. A test of usefulness is how it classifies objects. If you have done your needs assessment well, then you will be able to make a judgment about the usefulness of the program.

- Does the vendor give on-site training? How much training? Is there a fee for this?

- Does the vendor support the program either over the telephone or on-line? Do they charge for this? Check with the people on their client list on how well they do.

- In the case of proprietary programs, the program produced should be a "work for hire." That is, it is the museum's property. You should not be restricted in how you can adapt or use the program or which vendor you can use to update it. The original vendor may not be around when needed. Also, you do not want to pay a vendor the start-up costs to develop a program that they will market widely. On the other hand, the vendor may not want to create a program for you that you will sell or give away far and wide with no benefit to the vendor. You will have to reach an agreement with the vendor on this. I would warn you away from any deal where only the original vendor may update the program.

Do It Yourself

You have another choice. If you are familiar with computers, you may be able to adapt an application yourself. You become your own third-party vendor. This may prove to be an excellent way for a small museum that can define its goals and keep things simple. This is also a procedure that the museum has to approach very cautiously. I know several cases where someone worked on one of these adaptations for a long period of time, in two cases for several years, and never produced a useful program.[8]

The museum should have an agreement with the staff member doing this on the goals of the program, a timetable, and a measurement of success. Documentation (a user manual) should be part of the package. I would not get into this unless:

- The staff member is already familiar with programming or adapting applications. It is not a good idea for someone to learn to program on your time, and make all their mistakes in your museum.

- There is some mutually agreed upon measure of the success of the program. A simple measurement would be that the program answers the needs discovered in your needs assessment, be usable by any staff member, be able to do sophisticated searches (find all the bow-back Windsor chairs made in Hero County before 1800), be able to produce a certain number and type of reports, have a user manual, and data dictionary.
- The program can be finished in a specific time frame—usually no longer than a third-party vendor would take to develop the same program.

I adapted an application program at the Old Barracks Museum. I spent three months working with the old records and collection in developing an idea of our needs before I even bought the application program. This advance work would have been needed for any type of program selected. I had the museum's program created and up and running in about four hours, but then I had designed the program to use only one screen. I have updated it a little since as I found things had been forgotten or were never used. I have written a thirty-page user's manual with data standards for the system. It would have been a lot cheaper to buy one of the museum-specific programs, but the museum did not have the funds for this although they did have my salary. Of course, the Old Barracks now has a program that fits its specific needs.

Something to Think About

A third-party program will have been tried and tested for applicability in many museums and should be up and running within a few minutes of being installed, but it will be designed to fit the needs of a wide range of museums. The proprietary program may suit your needs best, match unusual hardware requirements, and include things that no other program has, but it will take a lot more money, time, and work. The small museum may find that it can keep costs down and usefulness up by creating their own program.

How to Make a Choice

The mass-marketed third-party museum software has a lot to offer small museums. You are in a much better position to evaluate it than any other program, the vendor will have a track record, you can see it in operation in other museums, and the start-up time is minimal. On the other hand, if the museum has needs that are specific to the museum, has unusual hardware requirements, and has to make complicated searches or produce sophisticated documents, then proprietary software designed specifically for you may be the choice. Finally, if you can enforce rigid standards, and the museum has a staff member familiar with data management systems, you may be able to write your own program.

Hardware

I have not discussed hardware very much. When you have made all the choices for your software you will find the choice of hardware is relatively simple. You probably cannot have too fast a machine, too much mass storage (disk), or too much memory, but the practical consideration of cost will govern that to some extent. It is a good idea to buy at least twice as much mass storage space as you will need, if not more. Three times would not be too much.

In dealing with PCs, I recommend buying only hardware that has a configuration, that has a wide popular acceptance—that is, it is made by several manufacturers, and that has well-understood industrywide standards. When you buy a machine with a configuration that only one manufacturer makes, then you are at their mercy, and software choices are more limited.

I am equally reluctant to buy software that will run on only one particular manufacturer's computer. This is so-called hardware-specific software. The program for a computer should run on all the machines in its class. Minis and mainframes may require hardware-specific programs. Even with these specialized programs, the data should be transportable, though you may have more limited choices.

LANs and WANs

If there are a number of computers in the museum, it may pay to set up a Local Area Network (LAN). If the museum has facilities scattered over a region, or is statewide or national, then you may need a Wide Area Network (WAN). These are two different kinds of applications, and may require different hardware and software than the other. These networks are usually very difficult to set up and will require an expert. There may be a saving to offset the cost of these networks as you will have increased ability to communicate, higher efficiency, may not need as sophisticated terminals for everyone, share software, printers, faxes, and scanners.

Enforcing networkwide discipline requires some sophisticated management techniques. If you install a network on more than two or three machines, you had better be prepared to spend some time on administrating the network. Both types of network require extensive security measures, particularly the WAN.

Data Entry and Testing

A program is useless until the data are entered into the data bank. Data entry is a real chore and it is where many computer projects go wrong.[9] The data in most paper records will not translate easily to a computer record. Until the data conform to specific standards they will not be very useful. There are several ways to handle this:

- You can develop a "Data Capture Sheet" that has a place for every field in the computer program. This is just a version of the Worksheet discussed earlier. You can update the data as you enter them on the form. Then inexperienced data-entry persons can enter the information into the computer. This may be the best method, but it will take a lot longer than other methods before you have entered enough data to be useful; an awful lot longer. See the example of the Data Capture Sheet (Figure 17, Worksheet).
- You can update the information as you enter it from the original records. This will require trained people to do the data entry, though they do not necessarily have to be the professional staff. They can be volunteers. I used this system at the Old Barracks Museum and found it efficient and produced usable data almost instantly.
- Or you can enter the data as they are and update them afterward. Untrained people can do the data entry, but a trained person is going to have to go through each record and correct it. This is a method that a small museum might consider as you get usable data almost from the start. There are "optical character readers" (OCRs) that may be able to read your old data into your new files. If you have a large collection file, an OCR may be worth exploring.

In any case, the professional staff is going to have to check each record. You can get the computer to do some of the updating for you or at least find some of the errors (such as all the objects without measurements).

You will need a "data dictionary." This sets standards for data. You might be able to tell the difference between "stockings, pair," "stockings, pr," "pair of stockings," and "stockings (a–b)," but a computer can't do this without very complicated instructions. With museum-specific programs, some of this will be decided for you. For other applications you will have to pick one way or another to enter data, and you must establish similar standards for each data field. On the other hand, you can make fields accept only certain types of data, or only accept certain words, or make the field conform to a standard, or automatically adapt the data to your specifications. This ability mitigates, to a limited extent, the need for rigid standards.

When you start up a program, it is a good idea to enter a few records and test the system. Enter about a hundred records and try it out. You will discover many of the problems of data entry and idiosyncrasies of the program. After you have a thousand or so records, you ought to do this again. A file of the latter size will also give you an idea of how much space the whole file will take up on your disk and an accurate estimate of the time required to enter all the museum records.

Hero County Historical Society

Title of object: **Accession number:**

Classification: **Old Accession Number:**

How acquired: **Pair or Set?:**

Source: **Location:**

Material: **Flag:**

Value: $ **How Valued:**   **Source of Value:**

Height: **Width:**   **Depth:**   **Diameter:**

Place of origin

Maker:

Association:

Date (of manufacture):   **Conservation priority:**

Description:

Compiler:

Comment:

[This form is just another version of the Worksheet adapted to a computer data bank. It would serve equally well as the screen for a computer program. It contains all the fields discussed in Chapter Eight.

If this form is the first step in computerizing the collection then this would be the last paper record of the collection and should be archived.]

Figure 17. Data Capture Sheet.

Many museums find that volunteers can enter data if they have some training. Entering data is the most expensive part of the project and using volunteers can save you a lot of money. Once the volunteers are trained, they are a pool of people who are familiar with your system and can do all sorts of jobs for you.

How Many Objects Do You Have?

An interesting question comes up when you begin to the enter data into a computer —how many objects does the museum have? Are such things as a pair of andirons, a pair of stockings, a cup and saucer, a fireplace set, or a chess set one object or several? In a paper catalogue they are often listed as one object, or at least, on one card. There is a lot of discussion in the museum field of this question with little resolution. How you treat this depends on what kinds of results you need from the catalogue. If you are just looking for a simple catalogue system, perhaps treating objects en suite with others as a single object will work. Because the computer itself can't make judgments on how to look at this kind of quandary, I favor treating each unit of a set as a single record (except pairs of shoes, stockings, and gloves). It gives you a better idea of the size of the collection, you can track condition of each object better, you can make more sophisticated searches, and you can better predict the cubic volume of the collection. That means when you have a chess set you do not have one object but thirty-four; the thirty-two chess pieces, the board, and the box the set comes in.

If you make an individual record for each object in a pair or set, you may want to add a field to indicate that this object is part of a pair or set. I have a field for pairs and sets that lists the accession number of the first object in the suite.

Cost

Suppose you have just recatalogued your museum's collection and face retyping two cards on each object in our 10,000-object museum. If it only costs you $1 to type a card, and you have two cards on each object, then you have $20,000 in catalogue cards alone, plus a ten- or fifteen-drawer file cabinet. Depending on the nature of the data, you can own a good computer and have all your data entered for about that much money.

Cards are usually typed on existing equipment one at a time by a staff person, and the cost does not appear as a separate line item on the books of the museum. You have to buy the computer, its supporting software, and do the data entry as line items. That makes the project appear as a huge cost. Averaged over the life of the computer, and the usefulness of the data, a computer system does not cost anywhere nearly as much as manually creating, maintaining, and updating a card file. This is something you should consider when making the choice between manual or computer records and when you update your files.

People tend to think of the hardware as the most expensive thing in the registration system, but the most expensive thing are the data. It costs a lot to create and maintain it. As an example, at the Old Barracks, we had less than $2,000 worth of equipment and software, but about $15,000–$20,000 worth of data.

Updates

It is a lot more complicated to keep the computer file up to date than the old paper records. You will find yourself spending a lot of time updating the records. One of the advantages of the computer is that an active updating process will make the system much more useful as time goes on.

While a good paper system is good for decades, the useful life of your hardware and software is about five years, if that. You will have at least three computer programs that will be constantly updated; the adaptation of the application program you are using, the application program itself, and the computer's system program(s). The hardware itself becomes obsolete with amazing rapidity. The museum should budget at least 15 or 20 percent of the total cost of the system each year over the life of the system just for updates. Occasionally you will need more.

Security

Although the security of the records of any system is important, the security of computer files is a serious concern. It is not difficult for a well-meaning person to completely destroy your data bank in a few minutes, and there are people who are not well meaning. For this reason, access to the computer must be limited to the few people who can be trusted not to compromise your data. Most data managers allow various levels of access to the files through a password system. It is an excellent idea to use passwords and security levels. There are various methods of checking updated files before they are inserted into the data base. It is best if only one person be allowed to authorize the changes.

When you are on a network, or can be accessed via modem, then you have some real concerns about security. There is probably not a security system in the world that cannot be bypassed by a determined person, but you can keep most people out with very simple programs. There is also encryption. Depending on how much access you are going to allow to your records via networks and outside access, I suggest setting up some sort of block that will restrict outside access to only those records, and those fields, that are public.

There are programs called "viruses." These are programs that ride into your system on the back of other programs or data and can completely corrupt your system. You should have an up-to-date virus protection program installed. There are also programs, sometimes called disk managers, that can rescue lost data in the case of mechanical or electronic problems and make your operation more efficient. You should have one of those installed as well. I once had all the programs on my hard disk destroyed by a virus, but I had a "disk doctor." It was able to recreate all my data files, but lost the programs, which are relatively easy to replace. I then installed a virus protection program—a case of locking the barn door after the horse is stolen.

The programs that operate your registration system are very important. The disks should be "archived," that is, locked up in a secure place along with your backups. A secure place is not only safe from pilferage but also of ideal climate, fireproof, and free of electromagnetic interference.

Backups

You never faced losing your whole registration system in a fraction of a second until you got a computer. There is no excuse for losing your data. You need to back up your files regularly on disks or tape. Two or three times a day is not too often. There is a kind of backup where the system verifies that it is a correct and complete copy. You should make one of those at the end of the day. It is a good idea to keep two or three day's worth of backups in reserve. In case of discovering badly corrupted data, you can then go back before the problem started, and rescue your files.

You should have at least three backups at the end of the day. One of the backups should be kept in a fireproof place in the museum, perhaps a safe if you have one, and one off site. You can buy programs that will back up your files, and most application programs contain some sort of backup utility. Even a small collection develops a huge computer file and you will probably need a tape backup or one of those large-capacity removable disks. Make sure you back up both your data and application files.

It is a good idea to make a paper backup periodically. This is a difficult question to decide and will be governed by the size of your collection and needs. It might take a day or more to print 2,500 records. A printing of only 10,000 records may take several days and be a stack of paper several feet high. You may not want to do this very often. There are computer service houses who will do this for you at a relatively modest cost if they have compatible software. Electronic backups can substitute for paper.

Remember something about paper records! They tend to last. Computer programs deteriorate over time and need constant care. Your application program may get so old it is useless (although CD-ROM files apparently will outlast paper, but your hardware and applications must be able to read them). Without your application program you cannot read your files. Printed on archive-quality paper a computer record will survive for a very long time. In fire-resistant cabinets, paper will survive almost any fire and a wetting, something a computer cannot.

Since a computer file is in a constant state of update you will want to keep a picture of your collection at a certain period of time. It is a good idea to archive a backup every so often. Once a year is usually enough, but also just before you make a major update, and other needs may require other solutions.

A Computer Has Uses Other than Registration

To a small museum the computer offers many other advantages in addition to its usefulness in the registration system. Even a very small computer can give you a sophisticated word-processing program (often with the ability to set type for newsletters, other publications, and labels), an ability to handle membership lists, an ability to schedule tours and events, a method of forecasting budgets, an accounting system, a data file for such tasks as fund raising and address lists, and many other uses. The small museum may need these things long before it needs to place its registration system in some electronic data form.

What Not to Do and When Not to Do It

Don't make a needs analysis. Go down to your local computer store and buy a data management program on its looks. Set up a data base without reading the manual. Start entering data from the first record at hand. Do not make a commitment of time to the project. Do not learn anything about computers, and never update your programs or equipment. I can guarantee that you will have some interesting moments. I actually have seen systems where this has been done.

Conclusion

The computer can perform some very sophisticated tasks for you very quickly and efficiently, but knowledge of the computer, software, applications, and practices needs constant updating to be effective. If you learned to type when I did (the 1940s), you learned a skill that will last your lifetime. A computer skill lasts about five years at the most without updating. You have to constantly update your skills, hardware, and software. A museum must take a very long view with a computer.

Whether you use a computer or not, you are still going to have to follow a set of practices similar to the ones outlined in this book. A computer offers a solution to many of the complications of a registration system, and I expect that most museums will have them before very long. Just remember, the computer is a tool just like any other tool and do not get carried away by the technology.

NOTES

1. I am going to use the word "computer" for a device that uses and manipulates data in an electronic form. There is no single source for computers in museums. David P. Williams, *A Guide to Museum Computing* (Nashville: AASLH, 1987) is about the only book on computers for the history museum available, but he recommends some practices that I think would not suit most history museums; Richard D. Light et al., *Museum Documentation Systems: Developments and Applications*, (London: Butterworths, 1986) shows the development of computer systems in museums worldwide. For applications in small museums, see pp. 163–206 and *passim*; Robert C. Chenhall and David Vance, *Museum Collections and Today's Computers* (Westport, CT: Greenwood Press, 1988) is dated but useful; Registrars, Committee, Mountain Plains Museum Association, *Computerized Information Management for Museum Collections* (1990) is short but useful; Andrew D. Roberts, "The Development of Computer-Based Documentation," Thompson, *Manual of Curatorship, op. cit.*, pp. 136–141; Sheila M. Stone, "Documenting Collections," Thompson, *op. cit,.* pp. 127–135 is mainly manual systems but is useful.

2. Lenore Sarasan and A. M. Neuner, comps., *Museum Collections and Computers: Report of an ASC Survey* (Lawrence, KS: Association of Systematics Collections, 1983) shows a systematic approach to developing a computer system in your museum. It is rather more complicated than you need, but shows the method of analyzing processes.

3. Planning is discussed in Thomas J. Orlowski, *Smart Selection and Management of Association Computer Systems* (Washington, DC: American Society of Association Directors, 1995), pp. 12–32.

4. Williams, pp. 104–106, and in his appendices shows several more sophisticated versions of a similar record.

5. The term "data base" is thrown around a lot but refers only to a particular type of data storage. A more generic term is "data bank."

6. Jane Sunderland and Lenore Sarasen, *System Checklist of Automated Collections Management Systems Features* (Evanston, IL: Willoughby Associates, 1987). Although meant to promote the Willoughby programs, this checklist gives a pretty good list of features that you might look for in any program.

7. It would be well if you showed the third-party vendor David Bearman and John Perkins, *Standards Framework for the Computer Exchange of Museum Information* (Silver Spring, MD: Museum Computer Network, 1993). The address of the MCN is below.

8. For a good example, see Paul E. Rivard and Steven Miller, "Cataloguing Collections— Erratic Starts and Eventual Success: A Case Study," Fahy, *op. cit.*, pp. 211–214.

9. Lenore Sarasan, "Why Museum Computer Projects Fail," *Museum News*, 59, 4 (January/February 1981), pp. 40–49; she is speaking mainly about mainframes, but the same problems cause failure at any level; also edited in Fahy, *op. cit,*. pp. 187–197.

The Museum Computer Network, 8720 Georgia Avenue, Suite 501, Silver Spring, MD 20910, keeps museums abreast of current developments in computers in museums. Their telephone number is (301) 585–4414.

Conclusion

Registration of the collection is one of the things that divides a museum from a mere assemblage of objects. It is important that the museum develop a collection policy and that procedures carry the policy out. The system should:

- Implement a set of policies that carry out the museum's purpose.
- Ensure that all the information about each object in the collection is collected and put into some usable form.
- Protect this information so that it is a enduring part of the museum's records.
- Leave a trail that will account for all actions.
- Make this information accessible to the staff and the general public.

In practice, all of this may require a great deal of work, at least to implement, but it is not beyond the capacity of even the smallest museum.

You cannot imagine the difference in public perception of a museum that has its collection well in hand and one that does not. In the former case, the public will respect the museum as an institution that knows its job and that can be depended upon to fulfill its mission and that objects left in its care will survive to the next generation. In the latter case, however, the perception may be of a rather quaint set of fumblers who live up to every caricature of museum managers.

The board and the public travel to other museums. They often serve as volunteers or board members at them. Professionals from other museums form opinions as well. The public talks with the professionals at the other institutions. They cannot help but make comparisons between your museum and the others. You want that comparison to be a favorable one.

If the registration system and care of the collection need some upgrading, the public will be very understanding if there is a grasp of the problems and a plan solve them. The public will allow you time to overcome problems. They will support programs that accomplish your goals. What they will not support is a continuation of outdated practices.

A well-thought-out program to bring your collection practices to the state of the art is part of the modern museum picture. I hope that this book helps you achieve this goal.

Introduction to Appendices

The appendices contain two collection care policies. One is for a volunteer-run museum. It has a basic simplicity that can be followed by almost any organization, no matter how small. The second is for a museum with a professional staff. It is difficult to write one of these manuals without knowing the least thing about your museum, so these manuals will need editing to fit your situation. I configured the first collection care policies for a manual system and the second for a computerized one. You will have to adapt them according to your needs.

Appendix C contains a number of forms that can be adapted to either a computer or a typewriter. The fourth appendix contains some information that you may find useful.

A Registration Manual for a Volunteer-Run Museum

Hero County Historical Society

The purpose of this manual is to create a policy and procedure to ensure that the Hero County Historical Society has a registration system that will develop a collection that will serve the purposes of the museum, that will register the collection properly, that will preserve all the information on each object, and that will be in conformance with the highest standards of the museum profession.

Statement of Purpose

The Statement of Purpose of the Hero County Historical Society states:
[The statement of purpose of the historical agency should appear here.]

[The organization may have a charter, a constitution, and bylaws. The portions affecting collections should appear here.]

[If there is a collection management policy statement separate from the above, that should appear here. A sample collections management policy statement appears below.]

To direct these aims, the Board of Trustees has adopted the following collection management policy.

[*Example*]

Collection Management Policy

The Hero County Historical Society will collect only those items related to the purposes of the Museum, for which it has an ultimate use, and that the Museum can properly store, preserve, and protect. There will be a Collections Committee with the responsibility for developing and implementing a set of registration and collections care practices for the Museum. The manual developing this will be the collections policy of the Corporation, and will contain the necessary procedures. At the annual meeting the Collections Committee will report for the Board's approval on the state of the collection and on all new accessions, loans, and deaccessions for the year. In pursuance of these policies the Collections Committee submits this manual to the Board of Trustees.

Respectfully submitted,
Collections Committee

Adopted by the Board of Trustees on _____ .

Collections Committee

There will be a Collections Committee composed of at least four members. The Chairperson of this Committee must be a member of the Board, but any member of the Corporation is eligible to serve on the Committee. The Committee will have the general supervision of the collection. The Collections Committee is a standing committee of the Hero County Historical Society.

Curator or Registrar

The Collections Committee, with the approval of the Board, may appoint a Curator and/or a Registrar, who shall be members of the Committee. The Curator will be responsible for the care of the collection, and the Registrar will be responsible for the care of the records of the collection. These people will serve an indefinite term at the pleasure of the Board.

Registration File Cabinet

The Committee will acquire a good four-drawer legal-sized fireproof file cabinet with a lock. The cabinet should withstand at least 1,700 degrees Fahrenheit for one-half hour and should have an Underwriters seal. The Committee will place all existing records in that file. It will become the "Registration File Cabinet." The cabinet should be kept locked at all times. The Chairman of the Collections Committee will have a key or the combination, and there will be a copy in the Corporation's safe deposit box. On the recommendation of the Committee, the Board may assign keys or combinations to other members of the Committee.

Registration and Accession File

The Committee will create an Accession File for each year. All the information on each accession in the year will be in this file. The Committee will create other files on the registration system as needed. These files will be kept in the Registration File Cabinet.

Acquisition

When a donor offers to donate to the Museum an item or items, the Committee will have him or her sign a Gift Agreement Form. No object may be taken into the museum unless this form is signed. There shall be three (3) copies of this form: one for the donor, one for the Corporation, and one (the original) for the Committee. All donors should be informed that items are accepted subject to the approval of the Board. The original form should be filed in the Accession File.

In the instance of a purchase, the bill of sale and all other documents will be placed in an Accession File. Before the Treasurer disposes of any canceled check, those related to collections should be placed in the proper Accession File.

No member of the Board of Trustees, or of the Museum Committee, may evaluate an object offered for gift. Where such evaluations are requested, the Society will confine itself to cooperating with a qualified appraiser, who is retained by the donor.

Accession Register

The Committee will acquire a well-bound record book for the Museum's use as a register. The first one hundred pages should be left blank to record the existing collection. At the beginning of the next page, the Registrar will write the year this manual is adopted _____ and columns for the accession numbers, types of objects, the source, and the date of acquisition.

The Committee will take the items existing in the collection at the time this manual is adopted and try to correlate them with existing records and list them in the Register in the same fashion as the new accessions, and enter them in the front of the Register. The Committee will be sure to record all accessions in the Register including the address of the source of the accession and the date of acquisition. All entries into the Register will be in indelible ink. The Register is to be kept in the Registration File cabinet. All measurements will be in the inch/foot system.

Accession Ledger

The Collections Committee will have the Accession Records typed on high quality archival paper and bound at some convenient interval, say each year. There will be two copies of the Accession Ledger; one will be kept in the Museum library under archive conditions; the other will be the use copy.

Accession Number

The Committee will assign the number one (1) to the first object acquired under the new system, the number two (2) to the second, number three (3) to the third, and so on.

At the beginning of each calendar year, the Committee will start a new page in the Ledger for that year, but the numbers will continue in series.

Only one person will keep the Ledger and assign numbers, and if there is a Registrar, it will be that person. No one may use a number unless the number before has been used. The number shall be placed on the object in the manner described in Reibel, *Registration Methods for Small History Museums*, or Dudley and Wilkinson, *Museum Registration Methods*. The number shall be placed on all documents associated with each accession and those documents filed in the Accession File.

Accession Record

Each object accessioned will have a Worksheet filled in on it. These are to be kept in the Accession File Cabinet until copied and bound in the Ledger.

Catalogue Card

The information on each Worksheet will be copied on to a catalogue card. These will be filed alphabetically by the title of each object.

Donor File

At the end of each calendar year, the Registrar shall make up a file of donors and other sources. The card file shall contain the donor's or source's name and the accession number associated with each name. Only one card shall be made about a donor.

Acknowledgment of Gifts

Each gift to the collection shall be acknowledged by the Collections Committee, either with a Gift Form, or by letter, thanking the donor for the gift on behalf of the Corporation. A copy of this form or letter, with the accession number(s) on it, shall be placed in the Accession File. All gifts displayed in the museum must bear the name(s) of the donor(s) in this fashion, "Gift of XYZ." From time to time, the Committee shall supply the Publications Committee with a list of donors for publication in the Newsletter.

Deaccessioning

It is the policy of the Corporation to deaccession as few items from the collection as possible. From time to time, the Collections Committee may wish to remove items from the collection for the following reasons: the item is not germane to the collection; it duplicates a better example; it is a fake or not as represented; its condition threatens itself or the rest of the collection; or the Museum cannot take care of the object properly. On the Committee's recommendation, the Board, with two-thirds of the total membership in attendance approving, may declare an item deaccessioned. The deaccessioned item should be sold at public auction, traded, or donated to another educational agency, or destroyed. No deaccessioned item may be conveyed in any manner to a member of the Board, a member of the Collections Committee, or to anyone holding a post of trust or honor in the Corporation. Funds acquired from deaccessioning must be used to purchase other objects for the collection, or to conserve items in the collection.

Loans

Loans to the Museum shall only be for the purpose of enhancing the Museum's exhibits. The lending party will sign the properly executed loan form. The loan will be insured, using the Museum's carrier. The loan will be approved by the Committee and submitted for approval to the Board of Trustees at their next regular meeting.

Loans from the Museum may only be made for purposes of display in an exhibit that enhances the Corporation's purpose. The borrower will sign a properly executed loan form. The borrower shall furnish proof of insurance or of financial responsibility. Loans from the Museum must be approved in advance by the Board of Trustees.

Objects may not be borrowed or lent for a period of more than one year, but may be renewed from year to year for a total period of three years.

Report to the Board of Trustees

The Collections Committee shall submit a report to the Board of Trustees, at the Annual Meeting, stating all new accessions for the year, all outstanding loans, the general condition of the collection, a statement of work achieved, and any other matter they deem necessary.

Copy of the Records

At the end of the calendar year, the Committee shall have the records for the year copied. This shall include all documents, pages in the Accession Ledger, and copies of correspondence. The master copy of this shall be kept in the _____. Another copy shall become the working record for the Museum.

Protection of Intellectual Assets

For the purposes of this policy, the intellectual assets of the Association consist of the images of objects and documents in the collection, the image of the Museum building, the images and content of programs, physical copies of objects in the collection, and similar devices. When permission is made to photograph, copy, or otherwise use this intellectual property, permission is limited to a one-time use for specific purposes. A blanket, long-term, or unlimited use of intellectual property may not be granted under any circumstances.

Ethics

All actions of the Board should be such that they avoid an apparent as well as an actual conflict of interest with any aspect of the museum operation and its collection. The members of the Board will follow the practices in *Code of Ethics for Museums* (Washington, DC: AAM, 1994) or the *Statement of Professional Ethics* (Nashville: AASLH, 1996).

Amending the Registration Manual

The Collections Committee may suggest amendments to this manual to the Board. Upon approval these amendments will become part of this manual.

* * *

The documents implementing this manual are attached as a reference.

Example of a Museum Collection Policy for a Museum with Professional Staff

Collections Management Policy and Manual
Hero County Historical Society Museum

This document contains the policy and practices governing the museum collection of the Hero County Historical Society.

This manual was developed by the Museum Committee consisting of the following members:

XXXXXXXXXXXXXXXXXXXXXXXXXX, Chairman
XXXXXXXXXXXXXXXXXXXXXXXXXX
XXXXXXXXXXXXXXXXXXXXXXXXXX

XXXXXXXXXXXXXXXXXXXXXXXXXX
XXXXXXXXXXXXXXXXXXXXXXXXXX
YYYYYYYYYYYYYYYYYYYYYYYYYY, Museum Director, ex officio.

January 26, 19XX

Statement of Purpose

The Statement of Purpose of the Hero County Historical Society as given in the charter which was granted in the Superior Court, County of Hero, the State of Franklin, April 16, 1896, is:

[Example]

"The purpose of the Hero County Historical Society shall be to investigate, elucidate, and publish facts on Hero County history; to preserve objects of historical significance; to receive contributions; and to encourage patriotism and public interest in history."

Subsequently, on the adoption of the new constitution of the Society on June 12, 1972, the Board added the provision that this Society be a nonprofit organization.

In the bylaws adopted on September 30, 1973, this provision provided for a Museum Committee to operate the Museum.

[Example]

"Article V, Section 7: The Museum Committee shall have the general oversight and direction of the Museum, and shall report to the Board from time to time on the condition of the Museum and the collection. The Museum Committee shall consist of a member of the Board, who shall be chairman, and of at least two other members in good standing of the Society."

Subsequently, upon employing a professional director, the Society adopted this clause to the bylaws on March 4, 1985:

[Example]

"Article XII: The Board may appoint a Museum Director and other staff and set their duties, conditions of work, and compensation. The Museum Director will have the general oversight of the Museum and be responsible for the Museum building, exhibits, program, collection, and shall have the direction of the staff. The Director shall be an ex officio member of all committees except the Nominating Committee."

Since the original conception of the Society and Museum did not foresee the present nature of our organization, and since the above clauses in our bylaws, as well as other clauses in our charter and constitution, as well as policies and procedures adopted as resolutions over the course of time, do not provide for a modern museum program, this Collections Manual supersedes all provisions in the Constitution and Bylaws of the _____ respecting the Museum and its collection and become the operating document for the Museum collection.

Collection Management Policy Statement

This collections management policy statement is intended to further define the clauses in the constitution and bylaws respecting the Museum collection.

[Example]

"It is the policy of the Hero County Historical Society to collect only those items for the Museum that were made and/or used in Hero County; or were associated with a person, place or event in Hero County; or, to a limited extent, are typical or representative of objects made or used in Hero County; and which are of a historical, cultural, or aesthetic nature; and which fall in the period of the founding of Hero County."

After complying with the requirements for changes to the constitution and bylaws of the Society, this manual was adopted by the Board of Trustees, Hero County Historical Society, March 26, 19XX.

* * *

Responsibility

The Museum Director is responsible for the Museum and is solely responsible for its collection. The Director will work with the Museum Committee to improve the Museum. He or she, with the approval of the Collections Committee, shall have the authority to accept acquisitions for the Museum collection. He or she shall have the sole authority to make or accept loans. The Director will, from time to time, recommend items from the collection that are to be deaccessioned. The Director will report from time to time to the Board on the condition of the collection. The Museum Committee will act as the liaison between the Board and the Director.

Computer and Data Security

The Director is responsible for all the collection records. He or she is solely responsible for assigning access to the records of all types. He or she will assign passwords to other staff as needed. The master password shall be kept in the Museum safe. The Director will archive the original copies of the data base application program(s) and such other application programs as may be necessary to extract data. The Director shall make a backup of the records daily. One copy of the backup will be kept with the computer, one copy in the museum safe, and one off the Museum grounds. A paper backup shall be made and archived every year.

All the registration records and software will be kept in a locked fireproof file cabinet with at least a one-hour rating. The cabinet shall be kept closed except when in use. The Museum Director is responsible for the security of this cabinet and shall have a key or the combination. A duplicate key or copy of the combination will be kept by the Secretary in the Society's safety deposit box.

Before adopting a new data management program, the Director will assure himself or herself that the data managed by this program are transferable to the new program.

Acquisition and Registration

The acquisition of objects should expand and refine the Museum collection and aid in carrying out the Corporation's purpose. The purpose of registration of the Museum objects is:

- to preserve any associations with historic events, places, or persons that an object may have;
- to promote the preservation of the object itself;
- to establish the Society's right of title to the object;
- to aid in the interpretation of the object; and
- to allow the Society to identify and account for every object in the collection.

Acquisition of an object is after the Director submits copies of a Justification for Accession Form, with a signed Gift Agreement or bill of sale, and any other pertinent document, to the Collection Committee for approval. The Museum will not accept a gift in which the Museum's use of the object, or the Museum's right to display or not display the object, is limited in any way, or if the Museum is limited in any way from breaking up collections. However, the Museum may occasionally enter into partial ownership arrangements, life tenures, limited ownerships, or any sharing of title or possession for unique items that will be significant additions to the collection, but only on advice of attorney and with the expressed approval of the Board.

Within reasonable limits, the Museum may accept restrictions on how the gift will be acknowledged when it is displayed.

[A section similar to this may be required if there is an existing collection.]

On adoption of this manual the Director will take immediate steps to see that every object existing in the collection has:

1. An accurate Accession Record and description.
2. A unique record in the Museum data bank.
3. A unique accession number.
4. All known documentary information known about the object filed in an accession file and identified by the accession number of the object.

[This section is required in all manuals.]

All new objects taken into the collection after the adoption of this manual will have the following:

Paper Records

1. A transfer of title document. In the case of gifts, a valid Gift Agreement. In the case of purchases, a valid bill of sale. Bequests must have a binding transfer from the estate.
2. A Justification for Accession Form.
3. In the case of gifts, an acknowledgment of gift such as a copy of a letter or a gift agreement form.
4. In the case of loans, a signed copy of the loan form.
5. A unique accession number permanently affixed to the object.
6. An accession file on each accession in a secure file cabinet.
7. Copies of all documents filed in the accession file.

Computer Records

1. A complete record on each object in the Museum data bank. This record will contain enough data in appropriate fields so that the Museum may easily extract the following information:

    a. Management data, or data that relate the object and the records to each other.

    b. Descriptive data, or catalogue information; data about the object that can mainly be acquired by examining the object itself, or from fairly simple research techniques.

    c. Historical data that place the object in a historical context with people, places, or events.

  2. The original equipment manufacturers' software for the system software, data man agement, museum record keeping, and any other pertinent programs.

Every object will have its own record, including sets and objects en suite with other objects.

The Director will acknowledge all gifts by a personal letter, or may request that an Acknowledgment of Gift be signed by the President.

Accession Number

Each object will be numbered with a unique accession number. The accession number will have a control number, which will be the last two digits of the year of accession (with the exceptions noted below). The second number will be the accession number. In each year the first accession will be assigned the number 1 (one), the second 2 (two), and continuing in strict sequence to the last accession of the year. The third number will be the catalogue number. The catalogue numbers will begin with 1 (one) for the first object in the accession and continue in strict sequence until all the objects in the accession have been numbered. If there is but one object in the accession, it will be given the catalogue number 1 (one).

An example would be the accession number 90.26.3, in which 90 is the year of accession, 26 is the accession number and is the 26th accession in that year, and 3 is the catalogue number and is the third object in the accession. In the year 2000, and thereafter, the Museum will add a 0 (zero) in front of the control number, thus 036.92.21.

In the case of the existing collection, the accessions that have known provenance are to be registered with this numbering system. All the objects with an unknown provenance existing in the collection at the time of the adoption of this manual are to be given the accession number 1 (one); in 1990 that would be 90.1.XX, etc.

Nomenclature

The Museum will follow the system developed by Robert Chenhall, *Revised Nomenclature* (Walnut Creek, CA, 1996), in naming objects and in classifying the catalogue. The nomenclature shall be confined to terms actually used in the Museum registration system. The computer registration system should be able to produce a lexicon of the terms used by the Museum.

Catalogues

The purpose of the Museum catalogue is to give the Museum easy access to the records and collection to aid the Museum staff in accounting. The Museum's registration report should be able to produce the following catalogues, either on screen or in written reports:

1. All the records by accession number in numerical order.
2. All the objects alphabetically by title.
3. A nomenclature.
4. All the objects by source. The report should be able to show the different types of sources (donor, purchase, bequest, etc.).
5. A priority list of conservation needs.
6. All the objects by location.
7. A listing of the value of each object and a total value for the listing.
8. The ability to pull up records by the object's association.
9. [Depending on the nature of the museum's program you may also wish to produce a list of objects on loan to the museum. Under number 6 above, the program should already be able to produce a list of objects on loan *from* the museum.]
10. The Museum should have the ability to make "string searches" to extract useful data from the file.

[*The number and types of catalogues will be radically changed if there is a computer. There may not be a catalogue per se, only the ability to generate certain types of records.*]

Measurements

All measurements are to be in the inch/foot system. Any computer application program that the Museum acquires must have the ability to convert these to the metric system.

Deaccessioning

The purpose of deaccessioning is to refine the collection so it will help carry out the Society's purpose.

The Museum will only deaccession objects from its collection for the following reasons:

1. Duplication of a better example.
2. The condition of the object threatens itself or the rest of the collection.
3. The object is not germane to the collection.
4. The museum cannot care for the object properly.
5. The authenticity of the object is questionable.

The Museum will not deaccession objects that have a known history related to our purpose, or that are from living donors, or were accessioned less than twenty-five years previously unless the object is deteriorated to a point where it threatens itself or the collection or its authenticity is questionable.

Moneys received from deaccessioning may only be used for purchasing new objects for the collection.

Using the Justification for Deaccessioning form, the Director will recommend that an object be deaccessioned to the Museum Committee. If approved, the Committee will make a similar recommendation to the Board of Trustees. On their approval, the object will be disposed of.

Objects may only be disposed of by a public auction, absolute destruction, or exchange or transfer with another historical agency with a purpose similar to the Society's. No deaccessioned object may be conveyed in any manner to a member of the Board of Trustees, the Museum staff, or anyone holding a post of trust or honor in the Society.

The Museum may exchange or transfer objects in its collection for which it can no longer care or which fit the other criteria of the deaccession process. These transfers or exchanges will be with other museums, or educational agencies that can properly care for the object. Any object received in an exchange must fit the Museum's collection policy. Exchanges and transfers must be approved by the Collection Committee and/or Board, as with any other accession or deaccession.

A note that the object has been deaccessioned will be entered on the accession record in red ink. Computer records shall be flagged to indicate the object has been deaccessioned.

Loans

The purpose of a loan is to enhance the mission of the Society. Loans from the Museum should extend the Society's purpose outside the walls. Loans to the Museum should augment the Society's purpose while increasing the effectiveness of the collection.

The Director has the sole authority to recommend that the Museum lend or borrow objects. He or she will not lend or borrow objects without a properly executed loan form.

The Museum may not accept or grant "permanent loans" or loans for a term longer than three years.

Loans to the Museum

The museum will borrow items for exhibit only using a properly executed loan form. The term of the loan will be one year. If the exhibit extends past one year, the loan may be extended for a year, on a year-to-year basis, but for no more than three years in total.

Loans to the museum will be confined to those objects for which the Museum can care under the same standards as its own collection.

A loan register will be kept on all incoming loans.

Loans from the Museum

The Museum will lend objects primarily for exhibition in another museum or to a qualified conservators for conservation. Loans from the Museum will only be made on a properly executed loan form. Loans may be made to other nonprofit educational agencies if the Director is assured that the object will be cared for and displayed in a manner which meets or exceeds Museum standards. Loans will be made only to institutions that have a standard of care equaling or exceeding ours.

The term of a loan from the Museum is one year. For extended loans, the period may be extended for a year on a year-to-year basis but for no longer than three years.

[The museum may wish to adopt a clause such as this if the museum has a number of permanent loans or unknowns in the collection.]

Permanent Loans and Unknowns

It is the Museum's policy to resolve any questions concerning permanent loans and objects with unknown sources as soon as feasible. Immediately after the first inventory of the collection is completed, the Director will prepare a list of permanent loans and objects with unknown sources. The Director will present this list to the Collection Committee with any comments he or she may wish to make. After consideration of this list, the Collection Committee may consult the Museum's attorney and report to the Board any recommendations they may wish to make. The eventual disposition of this class of objects will be made a part of this manual.

Photography of the Collection

The Director will have every object in the Museum, and all new acquisitions, photographed for identification purposes. The print and the negative will be filed by accession number.

Conservation and Storage

On adoption of this manual, the Director will immediately take steps to prepare a report on the conservation needs of the Museum. The Director will, from time to time, make recommendations to the Board on the conservation of certain objects. The Director will report on the condition of the collection in his/her annual report.

Each record of an object in the Museum registration system will be tagged with a priority number for conservation, where 1 (one) requires the most immediate attention, and 5 (five) requires the least. Objects in the 4 and 5 classification will be considered exhibitable.

Each object will be assigned a permanent location, and the object will be said to "live" at that spot. When objects are moved the new location will be tracked.

Inventory

The Museum will inventory its collection each year. The inventory will consist of an examination of each object and the records. The condition of each object shall be noted. Records will be updated as needed. The inventory list for each year will be filed in the Accession File.

Evaluations of the Collection

[*If the museum insures or places a value on the objects in its collection it should use the clause below.*]

At the time of accession, the Museum will establish a value for each object in the accession. These values will be used to insure the collection and establish a replacement value for loans from the Museum. These values will be updated, if necessary, during the inventory. These values are confidential and are to be revealed only at the discretion of the Director.

Appraisals

No member of Museum staff, or of the Board of Trustees, or of the Museum Committee, may appraise an object as to its monetary value, or give more than a qualified assessment of identity or age. The Museum will not pay an outside appraiser to establish a value on any object being donated to the Museum. In the case of gifts to the Museum, the Museum, when requested, will confine itself to recommending two or more qualified professional appraisers and cooperating with any appraiser the donor selects.

The director will not evaluate incoming loans but will depend on the owner to supply value. If the value is unknown, a suitable appraiser shall be retained.

Properties

The expendable noncollection property of the Museum or Society is not part of this policy or manual. It should be accounted for in a manner recommended by our auditor. Reproductions of authentic objects used in exhibits or demonstrations are properties and should not be accessioned. In the event a property is taken into the collection, it shall be accessioned in the regular manner and given the same care as any other item in the collection.

Ethics

All actions of the Board and the Museum Staff should be such that they avoid an apparent as well as an actual conflict of interest with any aspect of the Museum operation and its collection. The members of the Board and the Museum staff will follow the practices in the Ethics Policy adopted by the Board, [Date]. In cases not covered by the Museum's Ethics Policy, the Corporation will follow the *Code of Ethics for Museums* (Washington, DC: AAM, 1994) or the *Statement of Professional Ethics* (Nashville: ASSLH, 1996).

Protection of Intellectual Assets

For the purposes of this policy, the intellectual assets of the Association consist of the images of objects and documents in the collection, the image of the Old Barracks building, the images and content of programs, and physical copies of objects in the collection. When permission is made to photograph, copy, or otherwise use this intellectual property, permission is limited to a one-a one-time use for specific purposes. A blanket, long-term, or unlimited use of intellectual property may not be granted under any circumstances.

Access

The Museum will grant qualified researchers with legitimate research goals in mind equal access to the collections on a bona fide need-to-know basis. The Director establishes what the qualifications of the researcher and the legitimate goals are. Moreover, the Director may limit access to the object to specified methods of examination and to certain times. The Director may require a written request, stating which objects are to be examined, the method of examination, and the reasons for the examination.

The museum registration records are not a pubic record but should be considered confidential information. The Director may provide portions of the registration records to qualified researchers, but restrict access to donor, location, and value.

Other Types of Collections

[*This manual does not cover such items as books, manuscripts, anthropological specimens, etc., which have well-recognized methods of registration. If the museum has a large enough collection in these other areas, provisions for their care should be incorporated in this manual.*]

Public Document

This policy is a public document. A copy shall be kept in the Museum office and made available to any interested person.

Amendments

This Collections Policy and Manual may be amended by a resolution of the Board of Trustees following provisions in the constitution and bylaws respecting amendments.

* * *

The forms implementing this policy are attached as a reference.

Forms

It is necessary to have forms to make sure that:

- All the information is captured in an order useful to the Museum.
- Museum policy is carried out.
- There is an accounting trail so that all parties can account for their actions.

The trick is to have as few forms as possible.

With the computer being so ubiquitous, the nature of forms have changed. If the registration system is computerized, the need for most forms disappears and the ones used can be generated by the computer. In many cases, even such sacred things as ledgers and registers are kept in electronic form. Many forms now exist only as a particular screen in the registration program. Even in a manual system, the forms, or their format, are often generated by a computer in-house.

At one time I would have placed actual forms in this manual. These would be a guide for the printer when he made them up. The need for this has passed. I am going to present only a few forms in this appendix. For the rest of the forms, I will present only the type of data and the actual fields you should place on your forms. Whether this is a screen, a report generated by a computer, or an actual paper form will be determined by the nature of your registration system.

Many of the examples of how the forms are used appear in the text. The forms in this appendix are listed roughly in the order they appear in the book. They are numbered sequentially from C-1 (for form 1 in Appendix C). This citation is used when the forms are referred to in the text.

For more on forms see the following books: Dudley and Wilkinson, *passim*, was essentially written before there were computers. There are many forms shown in this work by museums that had excellent control over their collections with manual systems. Malaro, *Primer, passim*, shows several succinct forms. To please lawyers you might look Phelan, *Guide, passim*, for many detailed forms. There is a large assemblage of forms in Kenneth D. Perry, *The Museum Forms Book*, revised ed. (Austin, TX: Texas Association of Museums, 1990). John M. A. Thompson et al., eds., *op. cit.*; see especially Sheila M. Stone, "Documenting Collections," *ibid.*, pp. 127–135, as she has many forms following British practice; as does Light, *op. cit., passim*.

List of Forms

List of Forms in the Text

C-1 Certificate of Gift Form

The format needs to agree with the laws of your state, so it needs to be looked at by a lawyer. The form should contain these provisions:

1. The donor owns the object(s) and has the right to dispose of them.
2. The donor is freely giving them to the museum.
3. The donor is surrendering all rights to the objects including copyright and trademark (if he or she owns them).
4. The donor understands that the museum:
   - Will display the object at its discretion.
   - May not keep collections together.
   - Reserves the right to dispose (deaccession) the object at its own discretion.
5. There is a place for a signature from a responsible party from the museum.
6. There s a place for a signature for the donor(s).
7. There is a place for witnesses signatures, if required.
8. The date the form was signed.

[*If the copyright or trademark is not passed to the museum, or is restricted in any way, that should be noted.*]

It should be clear that the gift is to the museum. The use of this form implies that you are taking the object into your collection. It is the first step in accessioning the object(s). You should use another kind of form if you are taking the object in for purposes other than inclusion in your collection.

One should consult Malaro, *Primer*, 52*ff*, and Phelan, *Guide*, 273*ff*, before developing any gift agreement form. This form and loan documents should be approved by the museum's attorney.

C-2 Printed Acknowledgment of Gift

The Board of Trustees
of the
Hero County Historical Society
gratefully acknowledges
your gift to the collection of the Museum

[a short listing of the donation might go here]

Sincerely,

[*signed*]
President

This form should be printed on high-quality card stock with a matching envelope. For some reason, it looks better when hand-addressed with a postage stamp, rather than typed and metered.

A letter is even better. There is an example of one in Chapter Two on acquisitions. Some museums use both a letter and a form.

C-3 *Justification for Accession Form*

This form is handy as it gives collection committees some real criteria for accepting or rejecting accessions. It makes staffs justify why they want to add the object to the collection. Later on, it will serve as an answer to why the museum thought the object important enough to accession, should the question ever come up. These are the questions that should be answered on the form:

- Does the object have a provenance, coherent history, or identification linking it to the museum's purpose?
- Does the object duplicate another object in the museum's collection?
- What is the condition of the object?
    - Does it, or will it, need conservation?
    - What will this cost?
- Can the museum take care of the object?
- If the museum does not accept it, what will happen to it?
    - If it is sold on the open market will its history be lost?
    - Will it be destroyed?
- If the museum is buying the object, does its value reflect market cost?

C-4 Worksheet

If neatly printed on good paper, this form will do as an accession sheet.

Worksheet
Hero County Historical Society

Name of Object: Accession Number:
Classification: Old Number:
Source: Address:

Method of Acquisition: Date:
Special Terms of Acquisition:
Value: Authority: Date:
Location: Date
Physical Condition:
Conservation Treatment: Date:
Description:

Part of a pair or set?   Material:
Place of Manufacture: Date:
Artist/Designer/Manufacturer/Distributor:
User(s):   Date:
Place of Use:
Association with Person, Place, or Event:
Association with a Social, Ethnic, etc. Group:

Marking, Inscriptions:
Measurements:
Provenance:
Intangibles:
    Style: Social Function/Value:

Compiler: Authority, if different:
Comments:

This worksheet is an adaptation of fields suggested by the Common Agenda Data Bases Task Force (1989). If you are using a computer data base, some of these fields can be included in the description. The fields should be arranged in the order they are entered or typed.

C-5 Accessions Register

This register is for a manual system. It is used *before* the object is accessioned. Its main purpose is to keep track of numbers. It gives you a quick view of the whole collection. The example is from a three-number system. If the single-number or two-number systems are used, you will need to list every object.

Computer systems generate this ledger, if needed, *after* the objects are accessioned. An example of a computer-generated register is in the text.

Acc. No.	Objects	Source	Date
999.1	Set of china, ca. 1770–1800, 42 pcs.	Mary Jones (Mrs. Charles)	2/13/99
999.2	Plow plane, ca. 1880	William Carpenter	3/2/99
999.3	Tuba	Johannes S. Bach	3/21/99
etc.			

A log would be very similar to this, but kept in a stenographer's notebook. There is an example in the text.

C-6 Example of Typed Accession Ledger Page

February 19, 1975

Gift of: Mr. & Mrs. Loyal Descendent
(in the name of Noble Ancestor)
123 Beesom Street
Hero, PA 15555

75.11.1 *Machine, broom-making*: Consists of a rotating clamp held by a ratchet; clamp is hollow to hold broom handles; in back is device to hold wire, consisting of crank-turned square bar on which slides a wooden spool; whole meant to fit on bench; base vaguely L-shaped; whole painted black; 37 1/2 x 27 1/4 x 10 1/2 overall.

75.11.2 *Clamp, broom*: Consists of two iron jaws worked by a lever; jaws can be raised and lowered by a ratchet and crank mechanism on left; one guide (right rear) broken; whole stands of two pieces of wood to working height; molded on lip of jaws is "Pat'd Sep. 10, 1876"; painted black; 43 3/4 x 14 x 30 (less handle) overall; 34" to top of handle with jaws closed.

75.11.3 *Cutter, broom*: Consists of a tapered wooden trough; at small end is cutter of cast iron that pivots on one end and is worked by handle; a series of holes is drilled in cutter making legend, "W & D York Pa." meant to sit on legs (missing); painted black; 44 1.4 x 28 1.2 x 12 1/2 overall with handle down.

Note: The above items belonged to Mr. Descendant's great-uncle, William Jones (early 20th century), a broom maker, who built house at 123 Beesom Street in 1920.

acc/DBR/mc

This form can be generated from a computer data bank, if needed.

C-7 Catalogue Cards

Examples of catalogue cards are illustrated in Chapter Six. Keep in mind that catalogue cards are not the complete accession record, but just the information you immediately need. If necessary, the card should lead you to the proper record.

At a minimum, the catalogue card should have the name of the object and the accession number. The two examples give about the maximum and minimum information needed on catalogue cards.

Example of a Main Entry Card

Object: Plate, Dinner	**Acc. No.**: 52.2.1
Class.: 04 Food Service	
Source: Ivy Propan	
Material: Pottery	**Size**: 11.375 dia. x .875
Maker: Clews	**Place**: England
Date: ca. 1830	**Association**: Lafayette

Description:
Flat Bowl with curving sides; marly curves up; lip faintly scalloped; foot ring; underglaze blue transfer of landing of Lafayette over white ground; on bottom is stamp between two circles, "Clews Warranted safe [illegible]"; and, in underglaze blue, "The Landing of Lafayette at Castle Garden New York 16th August 1824."

HERO COUNTY HISTORICAL MUSEUM

Example of a Donor Card

Truck, Mr. & Mrs. Mack (Dorothy)
56.36
62.33
75.8
82.27
93.21

C-8 Inventory Form

Acc. Number	Object	Location	Comment

You use something like this when there are no records. If you use this form with good records you will have to do a lot of flipping through records as the objects will be arranged in the order you found them. There are better ways to do this than using this format. Moving cards from one drawer to another is one. If you have a computer, you can generate a list and check off items as found.

C-9 Loan Form for Loans from the Museum

The loan form should contain this information:

- What is actually being borrowed.
- The purpose of the loan.
- How the object is to be cared for if particular provisions are required.
- Method of transportation and who is responsible for arrangement and payment. The form should state that the museum is only responsible for payment for shipment to the named address.
- The conditions under which the object will be displayed.
- The exact location at which the object will be.
- The exact dates of the loan, wall-to-wall.
- The fair market value of each object.
- The type and nature of the insurance and who is responsible for it.
- A clause detailing conditions if the loan is terminated early.
- A statement about how the conditions of the loan are to be amended.
- A statement that the total agreement is contained in the form and attachments, and no other conditions apply.
- Special conditions.
- Conditions for protecting intellectual rights and controlling the use of photography.
- The name and signature of the responsible parties.
- Date of signatures.

An example of typical conditions for a loan follows.

C-10 Conditions Concerning Loans from the Old Barracks Association

The Old Barracks Association (hereafter "The Association") lends items from its collection only to museums, historical societies, libraries, other educational organizations, and approved conservators that, according to The Association, can comply with the conditions stated below.

The conditions, as stated on this form, and any attachments, represents the total agreement between the Old Barracks Association and the individual, institution, or agency borrowing the object(s) (hereafter "The Borrower"). No other terms are binding on The Association. The objects are loaned for the purposes and the times stated on this form. This form is not valid unless signed by a qualified representative of The Association.

The Borrower is required to have an all-risk fine arts insurance policy from an insurance company licensed to do business in the State of New Jersey on all objects included on this form, at the value stated, with The Lender listed as an additional insured. The Borrower will furnish The Association with a certificate of insurance with a 120-day cancellation clause.

Objects are to be displayed at the place designated and in the manner approved by The Association. All objects listed on this form are in the condition stated. Object(s) loaned will not be exposed to extremes of temperature, strong light, humidity, noxious fumes, etc., and are to be protected from handling by visitors. The Borrower is required to promptly report any damages to the object(s) in this agreement to The Association. The Borrower will not clean, restore, or conserve the object(s) covered by this agreement unless written approval is given by The Lender.

The Borrower may take photographs of the object(s) for record purposes. A single photograph may be taken of each object for a one-time publication in a catalogue or similar use approved by The Association. The Association is to receive a copy off all photographs taken of the object(s). No other photography, or any other form of reproduction or publication is allowed without the written permission of The Association.

The objects will be shipped via the agent and method stated on this form. Packing, crating, and shipping are the responsibility of The Borrower under conditions agreed to by both parties.

The Borrower will credit The Association in all labels, publicity, publications, and public releases of information unless otherwise directed.

The Borrower agrees to keep The Association informed in writing of all changes in address and ownership that affect this agreement. The agreement and the object(s) listed may not be transferred to a third party without the expressed written agreement of The Lender. In the event of a change in address and ownership The Association agrees to pay only the cost of shipping that does not exceed shipping to the original address.

This agreement may be terminated by either party thirty (30) days after a written notice has been delivered to the other party. A registered letter is considered adequate notice. The party terminating the agreement is responsible for the cost of shipping. The Association agrees to pay only the cost of shipping that does not exceed shipping to the original address.

This agreement may only be amended by written approval of both parties and such amendments must be attached to this agreement.

C-11 Loan Form for Loans to the Museum

The criteria for loans to the museum are pretty much the same as loans from the museum, only this time the lender makes the conditions the museum must follow. As a practical matter, this form will be used mainly with private lenders; other museums will insist that you use their form, which will identify most or all of the following:

- What is actually being borrowed.
- Description.
- Condition.
- The purpose of the loan.
- How the object is to be cared for if particular provisions are required.
- Method of transportation and who is responsible for arrangement and payment. The form should state that, upon return of the object, the museum is only responsible for payment for shipment to the named address.
- The conditions under which the object will be displayed.
- The exact location at which the object will be.
- The exact dates of the loan, wall-to-wall.
- The fair market value of each object.
- The type and nature of the insurance and who is responsible for it.
- The name and signature of the responsible parties.
- A clause detailing conditions if loan is terminated early.
- A statement about how the conditions of the loan are to be amended.
- A statement that the total agreement is contained in the form and attachments, and no other conditions apply.
- Special conditions.
- Conditions for protecting intellectual rights and controlling the use of photography.
- A place for signatures of responsible parties.
- Date of signatures.

An example of typical conditions for a loan follows immediately.

C-12 Conditions Governing Loans to the
Old Barracks Museum

The conditions, as stated on this form, and any attachments, represents the total agreement between the Old Barracks Association (hereafter "The Association"), and the individual, institution, or agency lending the object(s) (hereafter "The Lender"). No other terms are binding on the Association. The objects are loaned for the purposes and the times stated on this form. This form is not valid unless signed by a qualified representative of The Association.

The Association will treat the object(s) as they were part of The Association's collection. The condition of the object is as stated on this form or attachments.

The Association agrees to compensate The Lender, through The Association's insurance company, for any loss or damage to the object(s) up to the value listed on this form. If The Lender elects to maintain their own insurance, he/she must furnish The Association with a certificate of insurance for the value listed with a 120-day cancellation clause from an insurance company licenses to business in the state of New Jersey, with The Association named as an additional insured.

The term of the loan is as stated. The loan may be terminated by either party thirty (30) days after written notice to terminate is delivered to the other party. A registered letter is sufficient notice of termination. The party canceling the loan will pay for packing and return shipment, but in no case, will The Association pay more than the cost of shipment to the address named on this form.

The Association reserves the right to photograph the object for record purposes. Such photograph will be restricted to the files of The Association. A copy of such photographs will be given to The Lender. All other conditions concerning photography and publication appear on the face of this agreement or in attachments.

The Association will credit The Lender in all labels, publicity, and publications unless otherwise directed.

The Lender agrees to keep The Association informed in writing of all changes in address and ownership. In the event of a change in address and ownership, The Association agrees to pay only the cost of shipping that does not exceed shipping to the original address.

If The Lender cannot, or will not, receive his/her objects back within ninety (90) days after the termination of this agreement, The Association reserves the right to exercise a lower standard of care, and/or charge a storage fee, and/or to take title to the object(s) in a manner described by law. A registered letter to The Lender's last known address is sufficient notice of The Association's intention to return the object(s) in this agreement.

This agreement may only be amended by written approval of both parties.

C-13 Deposit Loan Forms

a Deposit loans are very much like any other loan to the museum except:

- The loan is for a maximum of 30 days.
- The Museum does not agree to pay for any damage of loss except in the case of gross negligence.
- Pickup and delivery is usually the responsibility of the lender.

The clause governing the conditions of the loan might read like this:

It is understood the object(s) listed on this form are left for temporary deposit at the Museum and the Museum accepts no responsibility for them, other than due care. The lender is responsible for pickup and delivery. The condition on the receipt is as noted.

C-14 Condition Report

Most museums won't have a conservator on staff who can give technical answers to one of these reports, so the form has to be tailored for the museum staff. The form should have slots that require a written answer, not a check mark, to all conditions. You need a form for each object. A form should require specific answers for these things:

- Catalogue description of the object.
- Whether this form is just a routine report of condition or reporting damage.
- If damage is reported, the nature of it, and where, when, and how and who first noted it.
- Any work required.
- Estimated costs.
- Accession number and name of object.
- Over-all condition of object.
- The condition of the finish.
- The condition of the structure.
- The condition of the materials making up the object.
- The condition of parts, and if there are parts missing.
- If there is a mechanism, does it work? Is it complete?
- How clean is the object?
- Is there any inherent vice?
- A listing of old repairs.
- Any recommendations.
- The date the form was completed.
- Who made out the form?

C-15 Loan Register

Loan registers are like other registers—they only need to contain enough information to help you find the right record. A typical loan register might look like this:

Hero County Historical Society
LOAN REGISTER

Loan No.	Object	Lender	Date In	Date Out

There is a comment on numbering loans in Chapter Three.

C-16 *Justification for Deaccession*

You have to document deaccessions very carefully and very thoroughly. This form can help all the parties involved visualize the reasons for deaccessioning and object. The form should contain these questions:

- Reason for deaccession:
    - Duplicates another object.
    - Not germane to the collection (does not fit the collection policy).
    - It is a fake, or not as represented.
    - It is in poor condition.
    - The museum cannot take care of it.
- Is the history of the object tied in any way to the purpose of the museum?
- Are there any restrictions on this object?
- Is the object part of a collection?
- Is the donor still living?
- Does the community have an interest in this object?
- What will happen to the object if it is not deaccessioned?
- What is the method of disposal?
- Place for all approvals, curator, director, collection committee, board, etc.
- Action taken.
- Date(s) of action.

Sources of Supplies Needed for Accessioning

Brushes, India ink, pencils, pens, Soluvar, etc.	Art supply stores or office supply stores.
Solvents	Hardware or paint stores
Soluvar, B-72, B-67	Conservation Materials, Ltd. P.O. Box 2884 Sparks, NV 89431 (702) 331–0582
Acid-free tape, paper, glues, cotton thread, etc.	Archive supply houses

Bibliography

[Note: The American Association of Museums will be referred to as AAM. The American Association for State and Local History will be referred to as AASLH. The International Council of Museums will be referred to as ICOM.]

AAM, *Code of Ethics for Museums*. Washington, DC: AAM, 1994.

AAM, "Ethics Codes: Past, Present and Futures," *Museum News*, 62, 2 (December 1988), p. 35.

AAM, "The High Cost of a Permanent Loan," *Museum News*, 66, 4 (March/April 1988), p. 38.

AAM, *Museum Accreditation: A Handbook for the Institution*. Washington, DC: AAM, 1990.

AAM, "Museum Positions: Duties and Responsibilities," *Museum News*, 57, 2 (November/December 1978), pp. 25–26.

AAM, Registrars Committee. Standard Facility Report. Professionals Practices Series. Washington, DC: AAM, 1989.

AAM, "A Code of Ethics for Museum Workers," *Museum News*, 58, 4 (June 1974), pp. 26–28 [The 1925 Code of Ethics].

AAM Registrars Committee, Professional Practices Subcommittee, "Loan Survey Report," May 1990.

AASLH Statement of Professional Ethics. Nashville: AASLH, 1996.

Association of Art Museum Directors, *Professional Practices in Art Museums. Report of the Professional Practices Committee*. New York: Association of Art Museum Directors, 1971.

August, Ramon S., "Museums: A Legal Definition," *Curator*, 26, 2 (June 1983), pp. 137–153.

Bearman, David and John Perkins, *Standards Framework for the Computer Interchange of Museum Information*. Silver Spring, MD: Museum Computer Newark, 1993.

Blackaby, James B., chair, Common Data Bases Task Force, "Final Report to the Field, September, 1989," Common Agenda for History Museums. Nashville: AASLH, 1989.

Blackaby, James C., chair, Common Agenda Task Force, "Managing Historic Data: Report of the Common Agenda Task Force," *Special Report #3*. Nashville: AASLH, 1989.

Brundin, Judith A. et al., "Inventorying a Historic Property," *Museum News*, 63, 1 (October 1984), pp. 17–25.

Case, Mary, ed., et al., *Registrars on Record: Essays on Museum Collections Management*. Registrars Committee, AAM. Washington, DC: AAM, 1988.

Chenhall, Robert G., *The Revised Nomenclature for Museum Cataloging: A Revised and Expanded Version of Robert G. Chenhall's System for Classifying Man-Made Objects*. Revised and expanded by James R. Blackaby, Patricia Greeno and the Nomenclature Committee. Walnut Creek, CA: AltaMira Press, 1996.

Chenhall, Robert G. and David Vance, *Museum Collections and Today's Computers*. Westport, CT: Greenwood Press, 1988.

Cook, G. R., "Should Curators Collect? Some Considerations for a Code of Ethics," *Curator*, 28, 3 (September 1982), pp. 161–171.

Deiss, William A., *Museum Archives: An Introduction*. Chicago: Society of American Archivists, 1984.

Dockerty, Janice, "What Is Unique About Historical Societies, *Registrar*, 10, 1 (Summer/Fall 1993), pp. 15–35.

Duboff, Leonard, "Copyright Law for Photographers," *Registrar*, 6, 2 (Fall 1991), pp. 1–13.

Dudley, Dorothy H., Irma B. Wilkinson, et al., *Museum Registration Methods*. Washington, DC: AAM, 1979.

Duggan, Antony J., section ed., "Collection Management," Thompson, *Manual for Curatorship, op. cit.*, pp. 113–376.

Fahy, Anne, ed., *Collections Management*. Leicester Readers in Museums Studies. New York: Routledge, 1995.

Feldman, Franklin, Stephen E. Weil, and Susan D. Biederman, *Art Law: Rights and Liabilities of Creators and Collectors*. 2 volumes. Boston: Little, Brown & Co., 1986.

Fore, Roland W., "Museum Collections: Access, Use, and Control," *Curator*, 18, 4 (December 1975), pp. 249–255.

Gallery Association of New York State, *Insurance and Risk Management for Museums and Historical Societies*. Hamilton, NY: Gallery Associates, 1986.

Graham, John II, "A Method of Museum Registration," *Museum News*, 42, 8 (April 1965). Also as AAM Technical Leaflet #2.

Guthe, Carl E., *Management of Small History Museums*, 2nd ed. Nashville: AASLH, 1969.

Guthe, Carl E., *So You Want a Good Museum? A Guide to the Management of Small Museums*. Washington, DC: AAM, 1957, reprinted several times.

Haines, Marsha S., "Partial Gifts: When Half a Loaf is Better than None," *Museum News*, 70, 4 (July/August 1991), pp. 68–70.

Hartman, Heddy A. and Suzanne B. Schell, "Institutional Master Planning for Historical Organizations and Museums," *Technical Report 11*. Nashville: AASLH, 1986.

Havermaeyer, Linden, "Old Loans: A Collection Management Problem," *Registrar*, 82, 2 (Fall 1991), p. 29.

ICOM Code of Professional Ethics. Paris: ICOM, 1987.

Lester, Joan, "A Code of Ethics for Curators," *Museum News*, 61, 1, (February 1983), pp. 36–40.

Lewis, Geoffrey D., "Collections, Collectors and Museums: A Brief World Survey," Thompson, *Manual for Curatorship, op. cit.*, pp. 7–22.

Lewis, Ralph H., *Manual for Museums*. Washington, DC: National Park Service, 1979.

Light, Richard, et al., Museum Documentation Systems: Developments and Applications. London: Butterworths, 1986.

MacDonald, Robert R., "A Question of Ethics," *Curator*, 31, 1 1994), pp. 6–9.

Malaro, Marie C., *A Legal Primer on Managing Museum Collections*. Washington, DC: Smithsonian Institution Press, 1985.

Malaro, Marie C. *Museum Governance: Mission, Ethics, Policy*. Washington, DC: Smithsonian Institution Press, 1994.

Manning, Anita, "Converting Loans to Gifts: One Solution to 'Permanent' Loans," *AASLH Technical Leaflet #94* (1977).

Manning, Anita, "Self Study: How One Museum Got a Handle on Collections Management," *Museum News*, 65, 6 (August 1987), pp. 61–67.

Miller, Steven, "Deaccessioning as Destruction" (Letter to Editor), *Museum News*, 69, 5 (September/October 1990), pp. 7–8.

Miller, Steven, "Selling Items for Museum Collections," *International Journal of Museum Management and Curatorship* 4 (1985), pp. 289–294.

Museum Documentation Association. *Practical Museum Documentation*, 2nd ed. Duxford, Cambridgeshire: Museum Documentation Association, 1981.

Nauert, Pat, "Glossary," Dudley and Wilkinson, *op. cit.*

Neal, Arminta, Kristine Hagland, and Elizabeth Webb, "Evolving a Collection Manual," *Museum News*, 56, 3 (February 1978), pp. 26–30.

O'Connel, Brian, The Board Member's Book: Making a Difference in Voluntary Organizations. n.p.: The Foundation Center, 1985.

Orlowski, Thomas, J., *Smart Selection and Management of Association Computer Systems.* Washington, DC: American Society of Association Directors, 1995.

Pearsall, Margot P. and Holly B. Uselth, "Registration Records in a History Museum," Dudley and Wilkinson, *op. cit.*, pp. 245–266.

Perry, Kenneth D, ed., *The Museum Form Book.* Revised Edition. Austin: Texas Association of Museums and Mountain-Plains Museums Association, 1990.

Peterson, Toni, director, *Art and Architectural Thesaurus.* New York; Oxford University Press, 1994, and other editions.

Phelan, Marilyn, *Museums and the Law.* AASLH Museum Management Series, Vol. 1. Nashville: AASLH, 1982.

Phelan, Marilyn and Robert H. Bean, *Museums and the Law: A Guide for Officers, Directors and Counsel.* Evanston, IL: Kalos Kapp Press, 1994.

Philips, Charles, "The Ins and Outs of Deaccessioning," *History News*, 38 (November 1983), pp. 6–11.

Porter, Daniel R., III, "Current Thoughts on Collections Policy: Producing the Essential Document for Administering Your Collections," *Technical Report 1.* Nashville: AASLH, 1985.

Porter, Daniel R., III, "Developing a Collections Management Manual," *Technical Report, 7.* Nashville: AASLH, 1986.

Pullen, Dennis R., "Inventorying Historical Collections in the Small Museum," *Curator*, 28, 4 (December 1985), pp. 271–285.

Rath, Frederick L., Jr. and Marilyn Rogers O'Connell, eds., *A Bibliography on Historical Organization Practices.* Vol. 4, Documentation of Collections. Nashville: AASLH, 1979.

Reibel, Daniel B, "The Use of Volunteers in Museums and Historical Societies," *Curator*, 17, 1 (March 1974), pp. 16–26.

Reibel, Daniel B, *Registration Methods for Small History Museums*, 2nd ed., rev. Yardley, PA: DBR Publishing, 1991.

Registrar, "Profiles: Janice Dockery," *Registrar*, 10, 1 (Summer/Fall 1993), pp. 15–20.

Registrars' Committee, Mountain Planes Museum Association, *Computerized Information Management for Museum Collections.* n.p.: Mountain-Plains Museum Association, 1990.

Registrars' Report, "The Role of the Registrar," *Registrars' Report* (now *Registrar*), 1, 1 (May 1977). Includes an interview with Irma B. Wilkinson.

Richoux, Jeanette A., Jill Serota-Braden, and Nancy Demyttenaere, "A Policy for Collection Access," *Museum News*, 59, 7 (July/August 1981), pp. 43–47.

Rivard, Paul and Stephen Miller, "Cataloging Collections—Erratic Starts and Eventual Success: A Case Study," Fahy, *op. cit.*, pp. 211–214.

Roberts, D. Andrew, "The Development of Computer-Based Documentation," Thompson, *Manual for Curatorship, op. cit.*, pp. 136–141.

Rose, Cordelia [Introduction], "A Code of Ethics for Registrars," *Museum News*, 63, 3, (February 1985), pp. 42–46.

Sarasan, Lenore and A. M. Neuner, comps., *Museum Collections and Computers: Report of the ASC Survey*. Lawrence, KS: Association of Systematics Collections, 1983.

Sarasan, Lenore, "Why Museum Computer Projects Fail," *Museum News*, 59, 4 (January/February 1981), pp. 40–49.

Stone, Sheila M., "Documenting Collections," Thompson, *Manual for Curatorship, op. cit.*, pp. 127–135.

Stuckert, Caroline M., Cataloging from Scratch: A Manual for Cataloging Undocumented Collections in Small Museums. n.p.: Caroline M. Stuckert, 1987.

Sumerville, James, "Using, Managing and Preserving the Records of Your Historical Organization, *Technical Report 9*. Nashville: AASLH, 1986.

Sunderland, Jane, and Lenore Sarasan, *System Checklist of Automated Collections Management System Features*. Evanston, IL: Willoughby Associates, 1987.

Thompson, John M. A., et al., eds., *Manual of Curatorship: A Guide to Museum Practice*. London: Butterworths, 1984. Section on collection management, pp. 113–376.

Toohey, Jeanette, "The Quandary: What Is a Curator," MAAM *Courier*, 13, 6 (November/December 1993), p. 4.

Ullberg, Allen and Patricia Ullberg, *Museum Trusteeship*. Washington, DC: AAM, 1981.

Ullberg, Allen D. and Robert C. Lind, "Personal Collecting: Proceed with Caution," *Museum News*, 69, 5 (September/October 1990), pp. 33–35.

Ullberg, Patricia, "What Happened in Greenville: The Need for Codes of Ethics," *Museum News*, 60, 2 (November/December 1981), pp. 26–29.

Ward, Nicholas D., "Copyright in Museum Collections: An Overview of Some Problems," *Registrar*, Part 1, 6, 2 (Fall 1989), pp. 13–19, Part 2, 7, 1 (Spring 1990), pp. 2–11.

Weil, Stephen E., *Beauty and the Beasts: Museums, Art, the Law, and the Market*. Washington, DC: Smithsonian Institution Press, 1983.

Weil, Stephen E., "Deaccessioning Practices in American Museums," *Museum News*, 65, 3 (February, 1987), pp. 44–50.

Williams, David P., *A Guide to Museum Computing*. Nashville: AASLH, 1987.

Zwiesler, Catherine, "Barcoding," *Spectra* (Museum Computer Network), 23, 1 (Fall 1995), pp. 18–20.

Index